Messiah REVEALED
in the FALL FEASTS

by

Hannah Nesher

Scripture quotations are taken from the Hebrew-English Bible. Copyright © by Bible Society in Israel 1996 and the Israel Association for the Dissemination of Biblical Writings. The Bible Society in Israel, P.O. Box 44 Jerusalem, 91000 Israel

Scripture quotations taken from the HOLY BIBLE, NEW INTERNATIONAL VERSION. Copyright © 1973, 1978, 1984 by International Bible Society. Used by permission of Zondervan Publishing House.

ISBN# 978-0-9733892-2-7

For speaking engagements please contact Hannah:

Hannah Nesher, Voice for Israel
Suite #313- 11215 Jasper Ave.
Edmonton, Alberta
T5K 0L5 Canada

www.voiceforisrael.net

Copyright © 2008 by Voice for Israel

All rights reserved under International Copyright Law. Contents and/or cover may not be reproduced in whole or in part in any form without the express written consent of the Publisher.

Cover design by James Vanderwekken - jvnderwe@hotmail.com

DEDICATION

To the God of my fathers, Avraham, Yitzchak and Yaacov,

יהוה
אהיה אשר אהיה

To You whose name says

You will be whoever You will be –

Thanks for being all I have ever needed!

And to Your Son and Messiah Y'shuah

ישוע

For your obedience to the Father

For being led like a lamb to the slaughter

For pouring out your soul unto death

So that I could live!

A Special Thank You

I would like to say *todah rabah* (thanks very much) and publicly acknowledge my debt of gratitude towards some of the many people who helped with this work.

First of all, to my mother and father who gave me life. Thank you for your courage in training up this daughter of yours through all our ups and downs. Although we may not always agree on theology, your love has remained constant.

To David, for applying your excellent technical skills to help bring this book to publication. Thank you for your love, encouragment and steadfast faith - and for the gift of our two wonderful children.

To my children, Clayton, Courtney, Timothy, Liat, and Avi-ad, who each supplied material and inspiration for my writing. Thanks for your patience with the crazy times in our family - for loving and forgiving me. Big hugs to Clayton for his great technical support.

To our ministry partners for your faithful love, fervent prayers and generous support. May you be fully rewarded by the God of Israel under whose wings you have taken refuge - Ruth 2:12

To James Vanderwekken for his awesome graphic design work and technical support. You are a treasure!

To Denis Vanderwekken & his late wife, Corrie for their friendship, support, and help in the journey. Corrie - I miss you!
To Marilyn for your intercession & willingness to proofread.

Most of all, to the Holy Spirit (Ruach Hakodesh), for giving me the inspiration, motivation, and words to write.

Todah rabah! (thanks so much!) תודה רבה

Contents

1	**Memorial of Blowing the Shofar**............................9	
	Happy New Year?...9	
	The Blowing of the Shofar....................................10	
	T'shuvah - Repentance...14	
	The Sound of the Shofar......................................16	
	The Need for Israel to 'Turn'...............................19	
	Prophetic Picture of Joseph.................................23	
	The Coming of the Messiah.................................24	
	The Rapture..25	
	God's Purpose in the Tribulation........................31	
	Days of Noah..33	
	Chronology of End Time Events.........................36	
	Book of Life..44	
	The Beast..49	
2	**Yom Kippur**..58	
	Atonement...63	
	The Arm of the Lord...67	
	The Narrow Gate of Life......................................69	
	When the Messiah Comes....................................72	
	Born Again - The Mikvah....................................74	

3	**Sukkot - Feast of Tabernacles/Booths**............83
	Z'man Simchateinu - Season of Our Joy......................83
	Schimini Atzeret - Last Day of the Feast......................84
	Scriptural Background to Sukkot..................................88
	The Real Thanksgiving..89
	The Prophetic Significance of Sukkot..........................92
	Tabernacles - Yeshua's Birthday..................................94
	The First Feast of the Millenium..................................96

4	**The Shelter of His Wings**................................97
	The Mark of the Beast..103
	The Help of Man is Useless.......................................106
	May Your Name be Inscribed in the Book of Life......110
	Leprosy in the Camp..111
	Supernatural Protection...113
	Running the Race..115
	The Shofar Call..116
	Added Insurance Coverage.......................................122
	Golden Kackie...124
	In the End..126

5	**God's Appointed Times**...................................128
	Citizenship in the Commonwealth of Israel...............128
	Temporary Blindness in God's Plan..........................130
	The Final Judgement...131

6	**The Relationship of Christians to Israel**..........134
	A Day of Vengeance - For Zion's Sake.....................135
	Intercessors - Watchmen on the Walls......................137

    Sharing Material Blessing..137
    The Unbroken Covenant..141
    Spiritual Adultery...142
    True Repentance Means Change................................144
    The Titanic & Grace..145

7   Simchat Torah..148

Postscript - Celebrating the Fall Feasts................................153

CHAPTER ONE

MEMORIAL OF BLOWING THE SHOFAR

(Zikaron Tru'ah)

HAPPY NEW YEAR!?

The so-called 'Jewish New Year' festival is unique. First of all, it is not really the beginning of the year. Secondly, we don't really know why we're celebrating it! Although most call this festival the 'Jewish New Year' and send New Years greetings to each other, much as Gentiles send Christmas cards, this is not actually the Biblical start of the year. In the Hebrew calendar Rosh Hashana (literally translated 'head of the year') occurs on the first day of the seventh month. Scripturally, however, the Bible designates the first month of the year as Aviv. This occurs in the spring when we celebrate Passover on the fourteenth day. Why the discrepancy? When the Jewish people were exiled to Babylon, they picked up some of the Babylonian customs, including names and dates. From Babylon, the names of several months were changed to their Babylonian counterpart. Aviv was changed to Nissan. Another change in the calendar originating out of Babylon is the change of the New Year to the seventh month instead of the Biblical first.

The Blowing of the Shofar

On the day of this festival, people in synagogues all around the world blow the shofar – the ram's horn - usually called the 'trumpet' in most Bibles. Why do we blow the shofar? Well, I suppose the main reason is because God commands it.

Biblical References to the Feast of the Shofar

> **"Speak to the children of Israel, saying: 'In the seventh month, on the first day of the month, you shall have a 'mini-sabbath' שבתון (shabbaton), a memorial of blowing of trumpets זכרון תרועה (ZIKARON TRU'AH)[1], a holy convocation.'"**
> (Leviticus 23:23-25)

> **"On the first day of the seventh month hold a sacred assembly and do no regular work. It is a day for you to sound the trumpets."**
> (Numbers 29:1)

"Blow the shofar in Zion." (Joel 2:1)

Our son, Timothy, at the age of nine blowing the shofar (ram's horn) in Jerusalem

---

1 Zikkaron Tru'ah-Remembrance of blowing ram's horn.

The Significance of the Blowing of the Shofar

Zikaron means 'remembrance' in Hebrew. What we are actually to be 'remembering' with the blowing of the shofar (the tru'ah) is a bit obscure, since scripture does not specify. However, the blowing of the shofar has several significant applications and purposes:

1. To hail a king
2. To call a solemn assembly
3. To sound an alarm
4. To warn of anticipated judgement
5. To gather troops to battle
6. To announce a new moon (Ps. 81:3)
7. To call for God's aid in battle against an enemy
8. To confuse the enemy camp (Judg. 7:19-21)
9. To celebrate a simchah (joyous occasion)
10. To proclaim liberty to the captives

The shofar, as fashioned out of ram's horn, may represent not only an anticipation of God's judgment, but also His mercy. It reminds us of how God spared Abraham's only son, Isaac, by providing the ram. As believers in Yeshua, we may blow the ram's horn to remind us also of God's great mercy towards us in not sparing the life of His only Son, Yeshua, in order to grant us eternal life. God, Himself, provided the sacrifice of His only Son in order that our lives may be spared.

> **"He who did not spare His own Son, but gave Him up for us all – how will He not also, along with Him, graciously give us all things?"**
>
> (Romans 8:32)

Biblical References to the Shofar

The shofar is being re-discovered by Christian and Messianic Believers all over the world as an effective tool in spiritual warfare. The Israelites were instructed to sound the shofar whenever they found themselves under oppression by their enemies. Then the Lord, when He hears the sound of the shofar, would 'remember' them and rescue them from their enemies.

> **"When you go to war in your land against the enemy who oppresses you, then you shall sound an alarm with the trumpets, and you will be remembered before the Lord your God, and you will be saved from your enemies."**
>
> (Numbers 10:9)

Joshua used the shofar, in accord with the command of God, to topple the walls of Jericho and conquer the city.

> **"When the shofarot sounded, the people shouted, and at the sound of the שפר shofar[2], when the people gave a loud shout, the wall collapsed; so every man charged straight in, and they took the city."**
>
> (Joshua 6:20)

Recently, there has been an emphasis on 'taking our cities for Christ'. Joshua knew the power of the shofar. When Gideon and his small, outnumbered, pitiful band of one hundred men blew their shofarot and broke the jars in their hands, the Midianites ran, crying out as they fled. (Judg. 7:19-21) We too may use the shofar, not only on the Feast of the Shofar, but at any time that we need victory in the battles we face in our lives.

---

2 Shofar - ram's horn.

The Prophetic Significance of the Shofar - the Re-gathering

The blowing of the shofar carries a highly significant prophetic message, especially to those of us who believe in the soon coming return of the Messiah Yeshua. Many of the ancient rabbis believed that it would be upon the blast of the shofar that the Messiah would re-gather His people from the four corners of the earth. The New Testament also gives reference to this global re-gathering of the Lord's chosen people.

> **"And He will send His angels with a great sound (tru'ah) of a trumpet (shofar), and they will gather together His elect from the four winds, from one end of heaven to the other."**
>
> (Matthew 24:31)

The prophetic purpose of Yom Tru'ah is to signal the re-gathering of God's people - to a pure faith in Him, as well as the re-gathering of believers to the Land.

> **"And it shall come to pass in that day that the Lord will thresh, from the channel of the River to the Brook of Egypt. And you will be gathered one by one, o you children of Israel. So it shall be in that day: the great trumpet (shofar) will be blown; they will come, who are about to perish in the land of Assyria, and they who are outcasts in the land of Egypt, and shall worship the Lord in the holy mount at Jerusalem."**
>
> (Isaiah 27:12-13)

According to the words of the prophets, this re-gathering is to happen when the Messiah comes. Therefore, we may look at this very day as God's appointed time for the return of Yeshua HaMashiach (the Messiah) and the return of the exiles to the Land.

T'shuvah – Repentance

The theme of the day of the shofar and atonement is repentance. It is not a time of feasting and celebration, but a somber period of critical self-examination. Most people take the day off from school or work in order to gather in synagogues to pray, listen to the cantor (worship leader) chant the Hebrew liturgy, and to hear the blowing of the shofar – the tru'ah. In the ancient world, the shofar was used to hail a king. So too, do we anticipate the day of our appearance before the King of Kings to face personal judgment. And yet, in all of this we hope in God's mercy and forgiveness when we come to Him with broken and contrite hearts.

> **"The sacrifices of God are a broken spirit; a broken and contrite heart, O God, You will not despise."**
> (Psalm 51:17)

Tashlich

Many Jewish people take the afternoon of the Feast of the Shofar to visit a body of water (lake, river, or ocean), to observe the ancient service of 'tashlich'. This custom is derived from Micah 7:19 where the prophet gives us God's promise,

> **"You will hurl all our iniquities into the depth of the sea."**

To illustrate this great truth and teach it to our children, we carry pebbles or bread crumbs to the water's edge and throw them into the water while reciting this verse and other appropriate verses about God's mercy and forgiveness. One year my husband jokingly gave me a big boulder to hurl into the river, apparently to representing the magnitude of my sins! For all those who feel they need a boulder rather than a pebble, remember that those who have been forgiven much also love much.

> **"If we confess our sins, He is faithful and just and will forgive us our sins and purify us from all unrighteousness."**
>
> (1 John 1:9)

The problem with sin is that so often, we just don't see it. The enemy successfully dulls our consciences, blinds our eyes to the truth about our sins. In pride and arrogance, we justify our sins rather than confessing them. The Word says that those who will not heed rebuke but harden their necks time after time will suddenly be broken, and without remedy (Prov.29:1). God in His mercy, does not want us broken beyond repair; He wants us to wake up out of our spiritual sleepiness and lethargy – to stop blaming others and finding excuses for our sins – to confess them in sincere repentance and find His forgiveness. The sound of the shofar helps us to do just that. The following is a devotional found in a traditional High Holy Day prayer supplement in an Orthodox synagogue:

Sound of the Shofar

May the sound of the shofar shatter our complacency
And make us conscious of the corruptions in our lives.

May the sound of the shofar penetrate our souls
And cause us to turn back to our Father in Heaven.

May the sound of the shofar break the bonds of the evil impulse within us
And enable us to serve the Lord with a whole heart.

May the sound of the shofar renew our loyalty to the one true King
And strengthen our determination to defy the false gods.

May the sound of the shofar awaken us to the enormity of our sins
And the vastness of God's mercy for those who truly repent.

May the sound of the shofar summon us to service
And stir us to respond, as did Abraham, "Here am I."

May the sound of the shofar recall the moment
When we stood at Mount Sinai and uttered the promise:

"All that the Lord has spoken, we will keep and obey."

May the sound of the shofar recall the promise of the ingathering of the exiles
And stir within us renewed devotion to the Land of Israel.
May the sound of the shofar recall the vision of the prophets,
Of the day when Egypt, Syria, and Israel will live in peace.

May the sound of the shofar awaken us to the flight of time
And summon us to spend our days with purpose.

May the sound of the shofar become our jubilant shout of joy
On the day of the promised, long-awaited redemption.

May the sound of the shofar remind us that it is time
to "proclaim liberty throughout the land
to all the inhabitants thereof."

May the sound of the shofar enter our hearts;
For blessed is the people that hearkens to its call.

A Wake-Up Call - Repent!

> "Wake up, O sleeper, rise from the dead, and Messiah will shine on you. Be very careful, then, how you live – not as unwise, but as wise, making the most of every opportunity, because the days are evil. Therefore do not be foolish, but understand what the Lord's will is."
>
> (Ephesians 5:14-17)

This feast is the time of year at which the warning goes out to the people of God – 'Wake up! Repent and turn back to God.' Wasn't this the message of John the Baptist?

> "In those days, John the Baptist came preaching in the wilderness of Judea, and saying, 'Repent, for the kingdom of heaven is at hand!'"
>
> (Matthew 3:1-2)

The chronology of the scriptures indicates that he began proclaiming this prophetic warning in the fall – at the time approaching the fall feasts. As Jews, they would have understood the timely message of t'shuvah (turn from your sins back to God). In fact, this prophet's name was not John, and he was not a Baptist. He was a Jew, whose name was Yochanan in Hebrew. He was not baptising, in the Greek sense of the word, but was immersing people in the waters of the 'mikvah'. This was, and still is a common Jewish custom of ritual purification. It is also used as the last step in the process of converting Gentiles into people who worship the one true God, יהוה YHVH, according to His Word – the Torah. He is the God of Israel, of Abraham, Isaac, and Jacob. He is the holy root, to which all people of the Lord must firmly attach themselves in order not to be swept away into the end-time deception, which is already upon us. Many people today are listening to false prophets who tell the people *"Revival is coming! There is no need to repent for one's sins – we, who are covered with the blood of Jesus are under grace, not law!"*

The Need for Israel to 'Turn'

Yeshua also came to His people Israel with a continuation of John's message: 'Repent – *turn back to God!*' Just as it is the sick who need the doctor, not those who are well, so is it the sinners of this world who are in desperate need to repent and receive forgiveness through Yeshua HaMashiach (the Messiah).

> **"Those who are well have no need of a physician, but those who are sick. But go and learn what this means: 'I desire mercy and not sacrifice.' For I did not come to call the righteous, but sinners, to repentance."**
>
> (Matthew 9:12-13)

Yeshua sees His people Israel as weary and scattered, like sheep without a shepherd, and He has compassion on them.

> **"But when He saw the multitudes, He was moved with compassion for them, because they were weary and scattered, like sheep having no shepherd."**
>
> (Matthew 9:36)

Even today, God as the good shepherd does not desire that even one of His sheep should perish but that they would repent and be saved. And yet, the Jewish people in Israel are being killed every day, like lambs given to the slaughter.

Today, a great tragedy is occurring in the nation of Israel.

Every day, Palestinian terrorists are murdering the people of Israel in bombings, shootings, stabbings, and other violent attacks. Why is God allowing this to happen? If God gave us this land in a divinely sworn oath, why would He give us over to the enemy like lambs to the slaughter? The whole country was plunged into mourning as twenty young Israeli teenagers were killed and almost a hundred more injured in a terrorist bombing in a Tel Aviv disco. This was soon followed by tragic accident in which a wedding hall collapsed and over two hundred of the guests were crushed by the rubble. This was the worst accident that Jerusalem of the modern state of Israel had ever experienced. We can't even blame this one on terrorist? Again, we must ask ourselves 'Why?'

T'shuvah

The answer is written in the Torah and it is simple. Repentance - t'shuvah. God promised to bless the people of Israel in the land; to multiply and prosper them and to give them victory over their enemies so that they can enjoy a safe, peaceful, abundant life in the Land. Anyone who has spent considerable time in Israel can testify, I am certain that the Israeli people are generally not enjoying these promised blessings of God for them in the land.

Why not? God promised the blessings but it was a conditional promise based on their obedience to His commands in the Torah. If they refused to obey His Torah, they would suffer the curses of the covenant.

> **"I will even appoint terror over you... and languish of heart...I will set My face against you, and you shall be defeated by Your enemies."**
>
> (Leviticus 26:14-17)

God even threatens to blot out the names of those whose hearts turn away from Him. (Deut. 29:20)

What is the remedy for the people of Israel in this deplorable situation? There is only one – repentance brought about by the convicting power of the Holy spirit. Jesus promised that when He went away, the 'Helper would come and convict the world of sin.

> **"Nevertheless I tell you the truth: It is to your advantage that I go away; for if I do not go away, the Helper will not come to you; but if I depart, I will send Him to you. And when He has come, He will convict the world of sin, and of righteosuness, and of judgment."**
>
> (John 16:7-8)

With repentence comes forgiveness found through the blood sacrifice of Jesus (Yeshua) the Messiah.

> **"If you return to the Lord your God and obey His voice…"**
>
> (Deuteronomy 30:1-6)

If the nation of Israel would turn back to God with broken and contrite hearts, and come into the New Covenant of forgiveness of sins, He would put all these curses on their enemies and on those who hate them. If we would turn back to God with all of our hearts through Jesus, He would give us victory over our enemies.

> **"Now thanks be to God who always leads us in triumph in Messiah, and through us diffuses the fragrance of His knowledge in every place…"**
>
> (2 Corintians 2:14)

Yeshua is the Torah; He is the living Word – the written word of God manifested in bodily form.

> "In the beginning בראשית (B'reisheet), was the Word, and the Word was with God, and the Word was God...And the Word became flesh and dwelt among us, and we beheld His glory, the glory as of the only begotten of the Father, full of grace and truth."
>
> (John 1:1, 14)

One day the Messiah will return to fight for Israel and Jerusalem against all of their enemies. At that time the nation of Israel, as well as the other nations will corporately mourn over their sins.

> "Behold, He is coming with clouds, and every eye will see Him, even they who pierced Him. And all the tribes of the earth will mourn because of Him. Even so, Amen."
>
> (Revelations 1:7)

This includes the people of Israel who will mourn when they finally look upon the one who was pierced in His hands and His feet and recognise Him as their Messiah.

> In that day there shall be a great mourning in Jerusalem... And the land shall mourn, every family by itself; the family of the house of David by itself, and their wives by themselves."
>
> (Zechariah 12:10-12)

The fact that the wives will mourn by themselves suggests that the group mourning will include the Orthodox Jews, who practice the segregation of the women for prayer.

What will be the response of Yeshua the Messiah towards

His Israeli brethren when He returns? Will He be so angry that they rejected and crucified Him that He will cut them all down in a mass slaughter as some Christians seem to suggest? We may look at a beautiful account of Joseph's reaction to his brothers as a prophetic picture of the Messiah's love and forgiveness towards His brethren.

A Prophetic Picture of Joseph

Most Jewish people do not recognise Jesus as their Messiah, Lord, Saviour, and brother. What is the reason for their blindness? The scriptures tell us that for a period of time, the Lord has placed a temporary blindness over the eyes of most Jewish people toward their own Messiah. The apostle Paul warns the Gentile believers not to be ignorant about the purposes of God towards Israel, and the part that this blindness plays in their own salvation.

> **"I do not want you to be ignorant of this mystery, brothers, so that you may not be conceited. Israel has experienced a hardening in part until the full number of the Gentiles has come in. And so all Israel will be saved, as it is written."**
> (Romans 11:25-26)

This ignorance would cause conceit or arrogance to prosper in the Christian Church, Paul warned, but unfortunately some of the Church has not heeded the apostle's warning. The fact that Israel will recognise Yeshua and will receive Him along with complete forgiveness and salvation is promised in the Word of God.

We can see the same prophetic picture in the Biblical account of Joseph. When his brothers came to Egypt, they did not recognise Joseph as their brother. Why? This Hebrew child of Jacob was all dressed up as an Egyptian. Today, Mashiach Ben David (Messiah

Son of David) has been dressed up as a Gentile to such an extent that His Jewish people cannot recognise this 'Jesus Christ' as their brother. They don't understand Him and are alienated from this blond haired, blue-eyed 'goy' (Gentile). But this was all in God's plan. Just as Joseph revealed himself when he wept and said to his brothers, *"Anee Yosef"* (I am Joseph) (Gen. 45:3), one day soon, Yeshua will say to his people, *"Anee Adonai"* (I am the Lord).

Not only will He forgive His people their sins, but He will also comfort them, as did Joseph towards His brothers, saying, *"Do not be distressed and do not be angry with yourselves, that you rejected Me because it was in God's plan for the salvation of many people."* Genesis 45:5(Paraphrase) Israel will be mourning upon His return, but after His judgment, we can expect a glorious reconciliation between the Messiah and His Jewish brothers as He kisses His brothers and weeps over them, just as did Joseph. What wonderful hope we have in our merciful God.

> **"Weeping may endure for a night but joy comes in the morning."**
>
> (Psalm 30:5)

The Coming of the Messiah

One of the greatest prophetic meanings behind the strident tru'ah, the sound of the shofar, is the return of the Messiah. One of the differences between traditional Jewish and Christian beliefs is whether or not it will be the Messiah's first or second coming. People who believe that Yeshua (Jesus) is the Messiah who came once to die for our sins and will return for judgment of the wicked, and to set up His kingdom on earth, anticipate His return. But Jewish people also anticipate the Messiah and eagerly await His coming. A story is told that a Jewish rabbi from Jerusalem said to a Christian pastor, *"Pastor, there is only one thing that I am going to ask the Messiah when He comes. Is this your first or your second time here?"*

The fact is that both Old and New Testaments give reference to the Messiah coming to earth with a great blast (tru'ah). And so on the Feast of the Truah, we anticipate the coming of the Messiah, and we may encourage one another with this reminder:

> **"For the Lord Himself will descend from heaven with a shout, with the voice of an archangel, and with the trumpet (shofar) of God. And the dead in Messiah will rise first. Then we who are alive and remain shall be caught up together with them in the clouds to meet the Lord in the air. And thus we shall always be with the Lord. Therefore comfort one another with these words."**
>
> (1 Thessalonians 4:16-18)

The Rapture

This event is commonly called the 'rapture', in which the 'saints', both dead and alive, will rise into the air to meet the Lord, much in the same way that Elijah rose into the air to be with the Lord while very much still alive. The rapture is a matter of great controversy in the Church. It is not so much the event itself which is the controversial issue, but the timing. Many Christians believe they will be 'raptured' before the time of trouble and tribulation that the prophets have told us will come upon the earth under the rule of the anti-Christ. But some believe that we will go through this time of terror and will only be lifted off the earth to be with the Lord when He actually returns. This is actually becoming a divisive battleground in Christianity.

Pre-tribulation Rapture Theology

Let me begin by admitting that there are many, many people, even 'the very elect' who will disagree with the view that I will present about the rapture. Many people today believe in what is called a 'pre-tribulation rapture'. Those who hold to this doctrine believe and teach that the second coming of the Lord has two or even three parts to it. In this scenario, the Lord comes for 'His Church' (those who are 'saved') before the tribulation and then returns 'with the Church' at the end of the tribulation. This means that the Church will not be on the earth during the rule of the Anti-Christ. An Orthodox Jewish rabbi, Chaim Richman of Jerusalem, speaks on behalf of Jewish people to express their feelings about this 'escapist theology'.

> *"We do not appreciate the idea that Jews are to be left behind and slaughtered while Christians fly away to heaven."* [3]

Batya Wootten, in her book, 'Who is Israel?' writes,

> *"Many who believe in a pre-tribulation rapture seem to think they will be eating wedding cake, while the poor Jews, who are left here on earth, will be going through terrible tribulation – until Yeshua comes back. And then, when the Jews finally* **"look on Him whom they have pierced"** *(Zech. 12:10) when they see Him, then, they will at last believe the same things the previously 'whisked away Christians' believed.*
> *"Certainly, the good rabbi's sentiments are well founded. All must agree that it is heartless to think*

---
[3] See Orthodox Jews Want Temple Rebuilt, Charisma Magazine, June 1993

> *of one group of God's people eating wedding cake while another is being severely afflicted – at the very least, such a scenario deserves to be labeled as bad party planning."* [4]

The Origin of the Theory

What is the source of this pre-tribulation doctrine? Men such as Clarence Larkin, C.I Scofield and J.N. Darby popularized this theory. Those who don't agree with this view are definitely in the minority, although our ranks are growing. And we need to keep in mind that the 'majority' has often proved to be deceived or incorrect in spiritual matters. We are never to follow the crowd blindly, but to search the scriptures for the truth.

What many pre-tribulation advocates don't realize is that Yeshua did not teach such a view, nor did the twelve Apostles or Paul. It is not found in any of their writings, but is a relatively new teaching, only having been presented since 1812 by a Jesuit Catholic priest.[5]

Edward Irving, founder of the Irvingite movement, known as the Catholic Apostolic Church, taught controversial doctrines in England and Scotland in the early 1800's. He was excommunicated by the London presbytery, and in 1833 condemned and deposed from the ministry of the Church of Scotland because of his teachings.[6]

He began to teach a 'rapture of the Church' after a young Scottish lass by the name of Margaret McDonald went into a trance and described a vision in which she said she saw the saints

---

[4] Arthur L. Watlins, '*Rapture or Transformation? Escape or Victory?*' vol. 7, book 4, (House of David Herald)

[5] Arthur L. Watlins, '*The Post Tribulation Rapture of the Church*', (Gulf Coast Bible Society, 3409 Alba Club Road, Mobile, Alabama 36605, USA).

[6] '*The Encyclopedia Britannica*', vol. 12, 1966, pgs. 648-649

leaving the earth at the return of the Lord, before the tribulation. Her 'revelation' was recorded in a book written by R.N. Norton and printed in London in 1861. Prior to this time, the Church, clear back to the Apostles, had always preached that the Church would go through the tribulation. There is no record of the 'escape rapture' theory being preached before 1830.[7] Irving accepted McDonald's revelation and his views influenced others whose writings and bible commentary popularized the theory. It was from this supposed revelation through a deceiving spirit, and not from scripture, that the modern pre-tribulation doctrine arose.

The Danger of Believing In a Pre-Tribulation Rapture

What is the danger in believing in a pre-tribulation rapture? If it is not true, but rather a major end time deception, then many sincere Christians, waiting for an 'any moment' whisking away from the troubles of this earth, are in for major disappointment and disillusionment, which may cause them to fall in their faith.

Bob Summers, in his book, 'Outback With Jesus', wrote of interviewing many Christians who have suffered persecution for their faith, such as behind the Iron Curtain, in Nazi Germany, and in Communist China. They all gave him the same urgent message:

> *"Go back and warn Americans that their moment is coming! Tell them they must get tougher – spiritually. And please tell them to stop preaching non-tribulation doctrines of escapism."* [7]

Some claim these to be false prophets. But the late Corrie Ten

---

7 Dr. Daniel Botkin, '*Left Behind*', Gates of Eden, Jan-Feb 2001, pg. 12, vol 7, no. 1, (PO Box 2257, East Peoria, IL 61611-0257).

Boom, whose true story of suffering for helping the Jews in Nazi Germany is told in her book, '*The Hiding Place*', confirmed their message. While in Jerusalem, she told the author of this article,

> *"Don't listen to these false prophets who come in the name of Jesus declaring that believers will not suffer tribulation! Go back and tell your American friends that the Rapture-Before-Tribulation doctrine is now an exclusive American message. It is not found in the rest of the nations. Christians the world over are already entering into tribulation".*

Corrie ten Boom went on to say that she had witnessed in many countries of the world where Christians were told, *"Don't worry, don't worry, you will be 'raptured' before the tribulation comes."* Then when terrible persecution came, the Christians were left scattered, tortured, and broken. The few survivors felt that God had forgotten His promise to come and get them.

A bishop from China later told her, *"Corrie, we failed God. We should have made the people strong for persecution rather than telling them Jesus would take them away from tribulation. Did Jesus say in the world ye will have no tribulation?"*

Corrie ten Boom, who watched her father and sister die at the hands of Nazis, and was herself imprisoned in a concentration camp for their aid to Jews in World War II probably knows more about the cost of true discipleship than the Christian whose bumper sticker reads, *"In case of rapture this car will be unmanned"*[8] An entire series of popular 'action' type movies and books, called 'Left Behind' have been produced now to promote the pre-tribulation rapture. It shows the entire world population of

---

8 Ibid.

Christians suddenly disappearing off the face of the earth – their clothes neatly folded in a pile at their feet. All who are left to face the persecution and horror of the anti-Christ are the sinners of the world. Unfortunately, these films and books are doing much to propagate this end time deception among the masses.

Deception

This is what the Lord Almighty says:

> **"Do not listen to what the prophets are prophesying to you; they fill you with false hopes. They speak visions from their own minds, not from the mouth of the Lord. They keep saying to those who despise Me, 'The Lord says: "You will have peace."' And to all who follow the stubbornness of their hearts they say, 'No harm will come to you.' But which of them has stood in the council of the Lord to see or to hear His Word? Who has listened and heard His Word? See the storm of the Lord will burst out in wrath…I did not send these prophets, yet they have run with their message; I did not speak to them, yet they have prophesied. But if they had stood in My council, they would have proclaimed My words to My people and would have turned them from their evil ways and from their evil deeds."**
>
> (Jeremiah 23:16-22)

In the end times, many will be deceived, even well known and respected religious leaders:

> **"False messiahs and false prophets will appear and perform great signs and miracles to deceive even the elect – if that were possible."**
>
> (Matthew 24:24)

It is not revival that is coming to the nations, but apostasy – a falling away from the faith:

> **"At that time many will turn away from the faith and will betray and hate each other, and many false prophets will appear and deceive many people."**
> (Matthew 24:10-11)

When is this time? During the time of God's testing and purifying His people on earth – the period of tribulation. During this time many will be: **"...handed over to be persecuted and put to death."** (Matthew 24:9)

God's Purpose in the Tribulation

What is God's purpose in allowing this time of trial and persecution to come upon His people? I believe that this period of time will accomplish the purification of His people. God wants all of our hearts, not just a leftover corner in a place crowded with other idols.

A story is told of a group of Christians worshipping together in a communist state, which forbad these meetings. Suddenly, the door flew open and there stood several soldiers with guns pointed at the group. The soldiers called out; *"Those who will deny Jesus to save their lives are free to go. You may walk outside to freedom. Those who will not deny Jesus even to lose your lives must remain."* Most of the group ran out the door to freedom, but a faithful remnant stayed behind, prepared to meet death in this life, but to face the Lord in eternal life. The soldiers shut the door, bolted it, turned around, and then laid down their weapons and said, *"Now we know who are the true believers here. Let's worship the Lord together!"*

> "Do not be afraid of what you are about to suffer.
> I tell you, the devil will put some of you in prison
> to test you, and you will suffer persecution for ten
> days. Be faithful, even to the point of death, and I
> will give you the crown of life."
>
> (Revelation 2:10)

Remember Daniel who chose the lion's den rather than pray to anyone but God? Remember Daniel's three friends who braved the fiery furnace rather than bow to a foreign god? How about Mordechai, the Jew, who refused to bow to Haman? These examples of Jewish men and women encourage us that we too will overcome this time of tribulation.

> "Him who overcomes I will make a pillar in the
> temple of my God...To him who overcomes, I will
> give the right to sit with Me on My throne."
>
> (Revelation 3:12, 21)

What about those who are not so steadfast in their devotion to God, but continue to walk in the ways of the world? God calls them 'lukewarm' and distasteful to him:

> "So, because you are lukewarm – neither hot nor
> cold – I am about to spit you out of My mouth."
>
> (Revelation 3:16)

Now is not the time to be lukewarm towards God and one's faith. It is time to listen to the blast of the shofar at this sober festival time, to hear the alarm and to wake up! Every one of us needs to seek God with all of our hearts at this time, and to repent of those things that do not please Him according to His Word and the witness of His Spirit.

It is during this time of trial and grave difficulty that the true believers will be sorted out from those who are merely lukewarm.

> **"Because of the increase of wickedness, the love of most will grow cold, but he who stands firm to the end will be saved."**
>
> (Matthew 24:12-13)

Today, we see wickedness rapidly increasing upon the earth. Recently, the headlines read, *"Newborn found in garbage dump"*. The former President of the United States faced impeachment for committing adultery and perjury. The blood of millions of unborn babies sacrificed to the god of immorality cries out to us from the earth for justice. In North American high schools, deranged students are murdering their teachers and fellow students; and raping young girls in the bathrooms.

Days of Noah

The evil and violence upon the earth is of such proportion that it can only be compared to the days of Noah. In fact, the Word tells us that the end can be compared to those days.

> **"The end will come like a flood."**
>
> (Daniel 9:26)

Despite the signs and prophetic warnings, most people continue on with their daily lives completely oblivious to or denying the coming destruction. I received a recent report that NBC produced a mini-series on Noah's ark. The television program turned the Biblical account of God's destruction of all life on earth (save Noah, his family and the animals on board the ark) into a slapstick farce depicting Noah and Lot living together in Sodom and Gomorra. But God will not be mocked:

> "As it was in the days of Noah, so it will be at the coming of the Son of Man. For in the days before the flood, people were eating and drinking, marrying and giving in marriage, up to the day Noah entered the ark; and they knew nothing about what would happen <u>until the flood came and took them all away.</u> That is how it will be at the coming of the Son of Man. Two men will be in the field; one will be taken and the other left. Two women will be grinding with a hand mill; one will be taken and the other left."
>
> (Matthew 24:37-41)

The emphases in the pre-tribulation doctrine are the phrases, 'taken away' and 'left behind'. However, if we read this in context, 'taken away' here means taken away to destruction in the flood. We may assume that 'one will be taken' also means taken away, not to glory, but to destruction. Yeshua also told a parable of the tares growing together with the wheat until the end of the age, at which time the tares will be plucked up and destroyed.

I believe that many Christians are making a grave mistake believing that they will all be 'raptured' or taken up into the clouds to be with the Lord before the time of tribulation occurs. This type of escapism theology is leading Christians down the dangerous pathway of apathy. After all, if we are not going to go through the tribulation, then we do not need to prepare for it; nor do we need to know the Word of God about it.

It is my hope and prayer that all those who believe in a pre-tribulation rapture or those who are not quite sure, will let go of all pre-conceived, treasured doctrines and allow the scriptures to speak for themselves. One of the reasons for holding on to this false doctrine is out of the fear of what we may be required to endure for the sake of our faith. Perfect love casts out all fear, and so with the perfect love of God in Messiah Yeshua, we bind any spirit of fear and cast it out. For there is nothing that can separate us from the love of God manifested in the Messiah Yeshua – not even the tribulation! Most of us have yet to experience that kind of great power and love of God that will give us the grace to go through the tribulation, but even in this we can trust Him to provide us with the grace and courage to overcome. God is faithful. As He brings us through trials and tribulations, He causes our faith to grow strong and our trust in Him to increase.

As we study the scriptures concerning the coming of the Messiah and the tribulation, we need to keep in mind Yeshua's words,

> "**These things I have spoken to you, that in Me you may have peace. In the world you will have tribulation; but be of good cheer, I have overcome the world.**"
>
> (John 16:33)

Whosoever Shall Lose Their Lives For My Sake

God did not 'rapture' Christians out of Nazi Germany. Many suffered; some even lost their lives. But for these, God has an eternal reward and this is our confidence and hope. If we are truly His, then the world will hate and persecute us (John 15:18-20). If we turn that around – if we are not hated and persecuted by the world, but rather its friend, what does that say about our walk with the Lord? In fact, Yeshua foretold that a time would come when whoever kills us will think he is doing God a favor (John 16:1-4).

Even now, many of the religious Jews in Israel persecute their Messianic brothers and sisters, try to pass legislation that would put us in prison, and some would even like to kill us as a service to God. We must be prepared not to protect our flesh or self-interest, for this is not the way of the cross. Yeshua told us to count the cost, and that whoever follows Him must also be prepared to walk that path. This requires our total commitment to our God and His Messiah, as did the Old and New Testament saints who went before us and are now a 'cloud of witnesses', cheering us on (Heb. 12:1).

Believers are warned not to seek to preserve their lives, but to be willing to lose their lives for His sake (Matt. 16:24-25). All who see martyrdom as something to be avoided have not yet gained an eternal perspective of their lives. They are focusing on a momentary earthly affliction, rather on the eternal reward, which awaits them.[9]

Chronology of End Time Events

In order to reveal the truth about the coming of the Messiah and the rapture, we must go to the source – the Holy Scriptures. Yeshua's own words to His disciples are clear concerning the order of events in the end times. Both the Old Testament and New Testament describe end time events. In the book of Matthew, Yeshua answers His disciples' questions about His return to earth. The following is a chronological listing of end time events with commentary.

1. Deception: Beginning of birth pangs of the Messiah False 'Christs' deceive many (Matt. 24: 5)

Today, in New Age religion and eastern mysticism, many claim to be 'Christ', or a manifestation of the 'Christ consciousness' within us. Signs, wonders, and miracles often accompany these claims, as the Messiah predicted. One Jewish believer, who was heavily involved in these false religions of demonic powers, gave

---

[9] Arthur Katz, (Ben Israel), *'Apostolic Foundations'*.

testimony of seeing a 'guru' manifest an image of a person on his palm, and then peel it off like a Polaroid. Tremendous numbers of people (including Jews who are spiritually hungry) follow and worship these gurus or false 'Christs'.

In Israel and around the world, a Jewish Lubavitch sect believes that Rabbi Schneerson, is the Messiah. It is ironic that Schneerson, who died several years ago and has never even lived in the Land of Israel but rather New York, and never fulfilled any of the Messianic prophecies of the Old Testament can be accepted as Messiah without anyone questioning his followers' identity as being fully Jewish. But we who believe in Yeshua as the Messiah are told that we are no longer Jewish and are, in fact, traitors to our people. Schneerson's followers proclaim him Melech Moshiach (King Messiah) on billboards, signs, and posters all over Israel. The sign below from a vehicle in Jerusalem reads, Barch haba (which translates literally from the Hebrew as Blessed is He who comes and is a form of saying welcome) Melech Hamashiach (King the Messiah). Yeshua said, "...for I say to you, you shall see me no more till you say, "Blessed is he who comes (Baruch Haba) in the name of the Lord (B'shem Adonai)." (Matthew 23:39) In seeing these sigsn in Israel, we thought, "Right slogan, but wrong face!"

Bumper stickers, signs, and graffiti all over Israel read, 'Na... Nach... Nachman M'uman'. This slogan is so prevalent that it began to drive me crazy! 'What does it mean?' I wondered. Finally, I found someone who would disclose the meaning – this is a chant that they believe all people will shout in unison when the Messiah (a deceased rabbi who was named Nachman M'uman) returns to Israel. Yes, the days of deception and false Messiahs are truly upon us.

Hebrew graffiti on a fence in Israel reads, "Nachman M'uman."

2. *Wars and rumours of wars, famines, and earthquakes* (Matt. 24:6-8)

Of course, we know that today, many nations have risen against other nations; famine plagues many countries of the earth, and earthquakes, as well as floods and other natural disasters have been increasing in frequency. These have only increased in severity and frequency since this time as God's judgement begins to fall upon the nations for their refusal to repent and turn back to God.

3. Persecution and martyrdom of God's true Believers

> "Then you will be handed over to be persecuted and put to death, and you will be hated by all nations because of me."
>
> (Matthew 24:9)

This corresponds with the Old Testament prophecies. Daniel received a vision of the end times in which a ruler would arise,

> "Who was waging war against the saints and defeating them until the Ancient of Days came."
>
> (Daniel 7:21-22)

This ungodly ruler will,

> "Speak against the Most High and oppress His saints and try to change the set times and the laws. The saints will be handed over to him for a time, times and half a time."
>
> (Daniel 7:25)

Again, this

> "...stern-faced king, a master of intrigue, will arise... He will destroy the mighty men and the holy people."
>
> (Daniel 8: 23-24)

If the saints, mighty men, and holy people have all been raptured, then who, exactly, is this ungodly ruler waging war against, defeating, and oppressing?

It amazes me how Bible-believing people can ignore these scriptures, I believe out of fear. I spoke once in a congregation on the end times, and after the presentation, a precious woman approached me and confessed that she had been praying that I would not speak about the 24th chapter of Matthew. It inspired fear within her, and so she ignored it, and yet this is the exact chapter that the Holy Spirit led me to speak about.

We need to deal with this spirit of fear within us and trust that God's grace will be sufficient for us to endure whatever He calls us to suffer. His Word says He will not give us more than we can bear, but we must now prepare by drawing so near to God; by developing such a close relationship with Him that we would be willing to give even our lives for our faith. It does not help us put our trust in the hope of a false rapture.

> **"Be faithful, even to the point of death, and I will give you the crown of life."**
>
> (Revelation 2:10)

4. The gospel of the kingdom will be preached in the whole world...and then the end will come. (Matt. 24:14)

Today we would be hard pressed to find a place in the whole world in which the gospel has not been preached. Modern technology and the sacrificial efforts of missionaries have made it possible for the message of salvation to be preached even unto the ends of the earth. Even radio stations such as the 'Voice of Hope' broadcasts the gospel from the middle of the sea into nations hostile to the gospel, such as in the Middle East.

5. The abomination that causes desolation will stand in the Holy Place (Matt. 24:15)

> **"So when you see standing in the holy place the 'abomination that causes desolation,' spoken of through the prophet Daniel – let the reader understand – then let those who are in Judea flee to the mountains."**
>
> (Matthew 24:15-16)

What exactly does the prophet Daniel say about this 'abomination'?

> "In the middle of the 'seven' he (this evil ruler) will put an end to sacrifice and offering."(This indicates the temple will be rebuilt and the sacrificial system restored) "And on a wing of the temple, he will set up an abomination that causes desolation, until the end that is decreed is poured out on him."
> (Daniel 9:27)

> "His armed forces will rise up to desecrate the temple fortress and will abolish the daily sacrifice. Then they will set up the abomination that causes desolation. With flattery he will corrupt those who have violated the covenant, but the people who know their God will firmly resist him."
> (Daniel 11:31-32)

At Chanukah each year (which by the way is *not* the 'Jewish Christmas'), we recount the historical record of the exploits of the Maccabees who resisted King Antiochus and his attempts to hellenize the Jewish community of Syria by forcing them to bow down to statues of Greek gods. Many Jews chose to be martyred rather than bow to a foreign god. Antiochus went as far as to desecrate the holy temple with statues of his gods and by sacrificing pig's blood upon the altar.

As bible believers know, the pig is one of the animals God declared unclean and forbidden for human consumption. (Deut.14, Lev.11) We are to detest its flesh and not even to touch it. Therefore, sacrificing a pig on the altar of God was an abomination and a direct challenge to His authority. The Maccabees miraculously defeated the entire Greek/Syrian army, drove them out of the temple and re-dedicated it to God.

What is this 'abomination of desolation' which will be set up in the holy temple? We can expect it to conform to the abomination that Antiochus set up in the past temple – statues of false gods and idolatry. Today, many 'temples' contain such statues and idols, but the worshippers don't seem to find anything contrary to the Word of God in such idolatrous practices. The anti-Christ, who will set up his statues and even the image of himself as God in the holy temple, will deceive these people.

> **"Don't let anyone deceive you in any way, for that day will not come, until the rebellion occurs and the man of lawlessness is revealed, the man doomed to destruction. He will oppose and will exalt himself over everything that is called God or is worshipped, so that he sets himself up in God's temple, proclaiming himself to be God."**
>
> (2 Thessalonians 2:3-4)

When this 'man of lawlessness' establishes a false peace and builds the temple, many will be deceived into believing that he is the Messiah. We must know that the true Messiah will only come in the clouds as he left.

6. A time of great distress (Time of Tribulation) - purification (Matt. 24:21)

> **"For then there will be great distress, unequalled from the beginning of the world until now – and never to be equalled again."**
>
> (Matthew 24:21)

The Lord further tells us that,

> "**If those days had not been cut short, no one would survive, but for the sake of the elect those days will be shortened.**"
>
> (Matthew 24:22)

Keep in mind that up until this point there is no mention of the coming of the Lord, nor of the rapture of the Church, but of the saints experiencing a terrible time of tribulation. Why would God bring this upon His people? It is for the sake of refining and purifying His people.

> "**Some of the wise will stumble, so that they may be refined, purified and made spotless until the time of the end, for it will still come at the appointed time.**"
>
> (Daniel 11:35)

The New Testament as well tells us that the Lord is returning for a bride without spot or blemish. The Messiah gave Himself up for a holy Church,

> "**To make her holy, cleansing her by the washing with water through the Word, and to present her to Himself as a radiant** קהלה **(Kehila)**[10] **Church, without stain or wrinkle or any other blemish, but holy and blameless.**"
>
> (Ephesians 5:26-27)

Daniel confirms this time of purification through the fires of tribulation in his prophetic word as well.

---

10 Kehila - Hebrew for congregation.

> "Many will be purified, made spotless and refined, but the wicked will continue to be wicked. None of the wicked will understand, but those who are wise will understand."
>
> (Daniel 12:10)

We cannot expect the ungodly of this earth to understand what is happening as we enter this time of distress, but those who know the Word of God should be well aware.

> "There will be a time of distress such as has not happened from the beginning of nations until then."
>
> (Daniel 12:1)

Deliverance – The Book of Life

And yet, we need not ever despair. In our God, there is deliverance.

> "But at that time your people – everyone whose name is found written in the book – will be delivered."
>
> (Daniel 12:1)

This clearly refers to the day of the shofar and the 'Book of Life'. The most common greeting and wish for this festival time is *'May your name be inscribed (written) in the Book of Life'*. Although most people do not accept the New Testament as a 'Jewish book', much of the richness of the text is lost without an understanding of its Jewish context. It's Jewish authors were certainly well acquainted with the Feast of the Shofar (trumpets) and the concept of the Book of Life. God is seen as judge, with a book containing all of our deeds – for good and for evil. It is believed that at this time of the year the Great Judge decides whether or not our names will be written in the book for another year.

When the thousand-year millennial reign is completed, Satan is temporarily released from prison for the final battle of Gog and Magog, after which the devil, the beast and the false prophet are cast forever into the lake of fire and brimstone. At this time, a book is opened, and the One who sits on the great white throne judges all the resurrected dead. This book which is opened is the Book of Life.

> **"And all the dead were judged according to their works, by the things which were written in the books…And they were judged, each one according to his works…And anyone not found written in the Book of Life was cast into the lake of fire."**
>
> (Revelations 20:11-15)

Faith and Works

Although Christianity has become a religion that emphasizes faith over 'works' to such an extent that 'works' has become almost a dirty word in Christian vocabulary, these and other scriptures show that our deeds have very much to do with our eternal destiny. James makes it clear that faith without works is dead and cannot save! (James 2:14-17)

Judaism is often unjustly criticized for being a 'religion of works', but Yeshua Himself says that when He returns, He will judge us on the basis of our works – what we have or have not done.

> **"For the Son of Man will come in the glory of His Father with His angels, and then He will reward each according to his works."**
>
> (Matthew 16:27)

Our name written in the Book of Life is our only ticket into the New Jerusalem. Only those whose names appear in this book will have the right to enter.

> **"But there shall by no means enter it anything that defiles, or causes an abomination or a lie, but only those who are written in the Lamb's Book of Life."**
>
> (Revelations 21:27)

It is possible, according to the scriptures, for our names to have once been written in the Book of Life and later lose this privileged position.

> **"And if anyone takes away from the words of the book of this prophecy, God shall take away his part from the Book of Life, from the holy city, and from the things which are written in this book."**
>
> (Revelations 22:19)

It is actually possible to have our names blotted out of the Book of Life.

> **"He who overcomes shall thus be clothed in white garments; and I will not blot out his name from the Book of Life, and I will confess his name before My Father, and before his angels."**
>
> (Revelations 3:5)

Only those who overcome and endure unto the end will retain their names in the Book of Life. So much for the eternal security doctrine of 'once saved always saved'!

We have need of endurance and even more so as we head directly into the end times.

> "Let us run with endurance the race that is set before us."
>
> (Hebrews 12:1)

It seems that the goal of most Christians is to be 'saved' and to get as many people around them as possible 'saved' too. But the scriptures have much to say about our eternal reward or punishment besides just making it to heaven. One day we will all stand before the judgment seat of the Messiah and we will be compensated for our deeds in this lifetime.

> "For we must all stand before the judgement seat of the Messiah that each one may be recompensed for his deeds in the body, according to what he has done, whether good or bad."
>
> (2 Corinthians 5:10)

It's not as if we just say, *"I believe in Jesus"* and then run the bases and we're home free. Or, as a pastor once said, *"Jesus is not simply a 'get out of hell free' card."* We will be required to give an account before the Judge of the Universe for the works of our lives. Only those works which are of Him – which originate from His divine inspiration and are completed in His strength will endure His refining fire. Nothing of our own selfish ambitions, performed to gratify our own self-interests and soothe our ego's insecurities will stand before a righteous God who sees the intents of our hearts. Even in 'religious works' we must ask God to cleanse us of impure motives, in order that we may gain the reward.

The scriptures speak of a resurrection of the dead, in which we all will be judged on the basis of our works.

> "Do not be amazed at this, for a time is coming when all who are in their graves will hear His voice

> and come out – those who have done good will rise to live, and those who have done evil will rise to be condemned."
>
> (John 5:28-29)

Yeshua's works stand, and His judgement is just, because He never lived to please Himself, but only to please the One who sent Him

> "By Myself I can do nothing; I judge only as I hear, and My judgement is just, for I seek not to please Myself but Him who sent Me."
>
> (John 5:30)

We, too, must allow the power of the cross to break our own selfish, self-interest and to live to please our Father alone. It is only with this expectation of eternal reward that we will be able to endure the coming times of distress. If we are still alive at the time of the coming tribulation, under the rule of the anti-Messiah, we may have to make the choice of whether to save our lives or lose them for His sake. If we can see in the Spirit, the reward that awaits us, God may grant us the courage to face even death with patience and even joy. For we know that those who are martyred for their faith win the privileged position of ruling and reigning with the Messiah after the first resurrection during the thousand year millennial period.

> "Blessed and holy is the one who has a part in the first resurrection; over these the second death has no power, but they will be priests of God and of the Messiah and will reign with Him for a thousand years."
>
> (Revelations 20:6)

The Beast

Those whose names are not written in the Book of Life will likely be deceived into worshipping this evil world ruler, the 'man of lawlessness' who corrupts through flattery and deceit. He is called 'the beast'. All who refuse to worship his image will be killed.

> "He also forced everyone, small and great, rich and poor, free and slave, to receive a mark on his right hand or on his forehead, so that no one could buy or sell unless he had the mark which is the name of the beast or the number of his name."
> (Revelations 13:15-17)

His number is 666. All the inhabitants of the earth except those who names are written in the Book of Life will worship the beast.

> "All inhabitants of the earth will worship the beast – all whose names have not been written in the Book of Life belonging to the Lamb that was slain from the creation of the world."
> (Revelations 13:8)

The Torah instructs us to tie God's commandments as symbols on our hands and to bind them on our foreheads. (Deut. 6:8) Many observant Jewish men take this instruction literally by tying a box containing the scriptures, called tefillin, onto their foreheads and wrapping the straps around their hands every morning. Our forehead and hands – our beliefs and our actions – are to be dedicated to God, not to anything or anyone that opposes Him and His kingdom of light. Scriptures tell us that one day, perhaps soon; all the inhabitants of the earth will be tested on this. The anti-Messiah will attempt to steal these places reserved for God by replacing them with his own mark of destruction. Those who refuse to take the mark will be placing their very lives at risk.

Martyrdom and Glory

Yeshua said,

> **"For whoever wants to save his life will lose it, but whoever loses his life for Me will find it. What good will it be for a man if he gains the whole world, yet forfeits his soul?"**
>
> (Matthew 16:25-26)

It is most likely that many of those who refuse to worship this 'false god', the anti-Messiah, will be martyred as were all our ancestors who chose death rather than bow to a foreign god. Jewish legend tells of a woman by the name of Hannah who had seven sons. They lived at the time of King Antiochus, during the period of the Maccabees. Hannah and her children were all lined up and commanded to bow to the statue of a Greek god. They refused. One by one, Antiochus' soldiers slaughtered Hannah's children before her eyes, until they came to the very youngest. The King urged the mother to instruct the boy to submit to the soldiers in order to save his life. The little boy looked to his mother for direction, and she said to him, *"Fear not this butcher, but proving thyself worthy of thy brothers, accept death."* And so, with this traditional last prayer on their lips, *"Hear O Israel, the Lord is our God, the Lord is One..."* (Sh'ma Yisrael Adonai Eloheinu, Adonai Echad."), both the mother and her last son were executed together.

Oh, that God would grant us the grace to bear martyrdom if necessary. For these, a great reward awaits – they will rule and reign with the Messiah for the thousand-year millennium – the time of perfect peace and rest. But he who would rather choose to save his life by worshipping the beast and accepting his mark, will

> **"Drink the wine of God's fury, which has been poured full strength into the cup of His wrath. He will be tormented with burning sulphur in the presence of the holy angels and of the Lamb. And the smoke of their torment rises forever and ever. There is no rest day or night for those who worship the beast and his image, or for anyone who receives the mark of his name."**
>
> (Revelation 14:9-11)

Everlasting Life or Everlasting Contempt

For most Jewish people the hope that their names are written in the Book of Life is just that – only a vague hope. However, for people who, by faith, have covered themselves with the blood of the Passover Lamb, we know that our names are, indeed, written in this book - not only for life in this world, but in the world to come eternally.

> **"For God so loved the world that He gave His one and only Son, that whoever believes in Him shall not perish but have eternal life."**
>
> (John 3:16)

Many people do not like to think about life beyond this world, but the Old Testament, as well as the New, clearly speaks about the resurrection of the dead, and two pathways – either everlasting life or everlasting shame and contempt.

> **"Multitudes who sleep in the dust of the earth will awake; some to everlasting life, others to shame and everlasting contempt."**
>
> (Daniel 12:2)

We have a choice in which pathway to choose, but time is quickly running out. The prophetic time clock is ticking loudly and alarm bells are going off all over the nations.

What is the fate of those whose names are not written in the Book of Life? The prophetic book of Revelation reveals that in the end, the books will be opened before the Judge who sits on the throne. The dead will be judged according to what they have done as recorded in the books.

> **"If anyone's name was not found written in the Book of Life, he was thrown into the lake of fire."**
>
> (Revelation 20:15)

We all need to make sure, right at this moment, that our names are truly written in the Lamb's Book of Life through faith in the atonement He made for our sins through the sacrifice of His own life. Why not pray now and put your faith in the salvation of your soul provided through Yeshua (Jesus) the Messiah, the Lamb of God. It is not enough to just 'live a good life and try to be a good person'. When the angel of death came to strike down all the firstborn of Egypt, he did not knock on each door to check if everyone in that household had been 'good enough'. They were only saved by applying, in faith, the blood of the Passover lamb to the door-posts of their homes.

When John saw Yeshua, he said,

> **"Look, the Lamb of God, who takes away the sin of the world!"**
>
> (John 1:29)

Only the blood of the lamb (Yeshua) is powerful enough to protect us from the wrath of God that is coming upon the earth.

7. The Second Coming of the Lord (Immediately After the Distress) (Matt. 24:30)

> "**Immediately AFTER the distress of those days the sun will be darkened and the moon will not give its light... At that time the sign of the Son of Man will appear in the sky, and all the nations of the earth will mourn. They will see the Son of Man coming on the clouds of the sky, with power and great glory.**"
>
> (Matthew 24:29-30)

These scriptures clarify the truth that the Lord does not return until after the time of distress and tribulation.

8. The Shofar will Sound – Resurrection and Rapture (Matt. 24:31)

After the Son of Man appears coming on the clouds and every eye sees Him, the people of the earth will mourn, realising finally who He really is and bitterly regretting their rebellion. The Lord will then send forth his angels with a loud blast of the shofar, and they will gather His elect from the four winds, from one end of the heavens to the other. (Matt. 24:31) When will this happen? No one really knows except the Father, but we are to be ready. Those who are watching world events through prophetic eyes can perceive key events now falling into place – the growing movement towards a one-world government, economy, and religion is gathering momentum towards the 'New World Order of the New Age'.

Time is short:

> "For the Lord himself will come down from heaven, with a loud command, with the voice of the archangel and with the shofar call of God, and the dead in Messiah will rise first. After that, we who are still alive and are left will be caught up together with them in the clouds to meet the Lord in the air. And so we will be with the Lord forever. Therefore encourage each other with these words."
>
> (1 Thessalonians 4:16-18)

This, then, is the long-awaited and hoped for rapture, but it does not occur until the Lord appears and begins His descent from heaven. The dead will first be resurrected, and then any believers who are left still alive on earth – those who have not been martyred – will rise up to meet the Lord in the air as He continues His descent to earth.

The Last Shofar

One other significant scripture reveals when the Lord will return for His people.

> "Listen, I tell you a mystery: we will not all sleep, but we will all be changed – in a flash, in the twinkling of an eye, <u>at the last shofar</u>. For the shofar will sound, the dead will be raised imperishable, and we will be changed."
>
> (1 Corinthians 15:51-52)

When will the dead be raised and the people of God changed into their imperishable bodies? At the last shofar. When is the last shofar? Chapters 8-11 of the book of Revelation describe the sounding of the seven shofarot (plural for shofar). Accompanying each shofar blast, a plague is poured out upon the earth. These plagues are very similar to the ones God used to judge Egypt. What will happen to God's people during the plagues? I believe God will extend His protection over them in a supernatural way, as He did with the Israelites in Egypt.

I will make a distinction…My People

Before we enjoy the time of the Messianic Age, of perfect peace and rest, we must endure the process of purification through the tribulation. If the children of God are not 'raptured' out of this terrible time of distress, what will happen to them when God pours out His plagues upon the earth?

If we look at the pattern God set in the Old Testament as a foreshadowing of what was to come, God did not remove His people Israel, during His pouring out of the ten plagues upon Egypt. Instead, He protected them because they were marked and sealed as belonging to God, and ultimately saved from God's wrath by the blood of the lamb. God repeatedly made a distinction between 'My people' and 'Not My people'. At this time, Israel was (and still is) in covenant with God as His special treasured possession, the apple of His eye. (Zech. 2:8) It is not that God did not love the Egyptians, but that at this time, they worshipped false gods and pagan deities. Their sorcerers and magicians performed signs and wonders but with a power that was not of God. The Lord executed judgment upon the Egyptians and upon all the gods of Egypt to prove that He is the one true God of all mankind. It is for this same purpose that He is preparing to pour out His plagues upon the world today.

God has the ability to protect His covenant people, just as He did with the Israelites in Egypt, even while pouring out His wrath and vengeance upon those who refuse to humble themselves before Him.

> "See, the Lord is going to lay waste the earth and devastate it; He will ruin its face and scatter its inhabitants... The earth will be completely laid waste and totally plundered."
>
> (Isaiah 24:1-3)

Why is the Lord going to destroy the earth? Because of disobedience to His laws.

> "The earth is defiled by its people; they have disobeyed the laws, violated the statutes and broken the everlasting covenant. Therefore a curse consumes the earth; its people must bear their guilt. Therefore earth's inhabitants are burned up, and very few are left."
>
> (Isaiah 24: 5-6)

But God is a God of Love!

Upon the blast of the shofar, the Lord's return will bring salvation and reward to all those living and dead, whose names are written in the Lamb's Book of Life, but those whose names do not appear in this book will be forever punished and separated from God.

> "Multitudes who sleep in the dust of the earth will awake; some to everlasting life, others to shame and everlasting contempt."
>
> (Daniel 12:2)

> "This is how it will be at the end of the age. The angels will come and separate the wicked from the righteous and throw them into the fiery furnace, where there will be weeping and gnashing of teeth."
>
> (Matthew 13:49-50)

Many people today are appalled at the thought that God will judge the earth and bring punishment or destruction. They say, *"God would never do that, He is a God of love"*. They have been taught about the love of God, but never about the justice of God. New Age philosophies tell us that if we just think positive thoughts, everything will transform into love and beauty, and nothing negative will happen. This completely disregards the truth that God is the potter and we are the clay, as well as denying the historical record of God's dealings with man in the bible. Some charge God with cruelty for His judgment, but He has given us free will - the choice of life or death.

> **"The soul who sins is the one who will die...He follows My decrees and faithfully keeps My laws. That man is righteous; he will surely live."**
>
> (Ezekiel 18:4, 9)

We were made righteous through the blood of Yeshua (2Cor. 5:21) It is not God's will for even one to perish, but to repent and live.

> **"Repent! Turn away from all your offences; then sin will not be your downfall. Rid yourselves of all the offences you have committed, and get a new heart and a new spirit. Why will you die, O house of Israel? For I take no pleasure in the death of anyone, declares the Sovereign Lord. Repent and live!"**
>
> (Ezekiel 18:30-32)

Repentance to salvation is the true message of the Fall Feasts.

CHAPTER TWO

YOM KIPPUR
DAY OF ATONEMENT

A Holy Day

Yom Kippur is traditionally considered the holiest day of the year in the biblical calendar. White, the symbol of purity, is the dominant color of Yom Kippur. All coverings used in religious services are changed to white, the rabbis and cantor as well as many people wear white and in some congregations all the men wear white skullcaps (kippot). White curtains cover the Holy Ark where the Torah Scrolls are kept. The inscription on the curtain quoting the prophet Isaiah supports confidence that the sins of the people will be forgiven.

> **"Though your sins be as scarlet, they shall be white as snow."**
>
> (Isaiah 1:18)

Even die-hard secular Israelis respect the holiness of this day in some sense. Since driving is prohibited on 'Sabbaths', Yom Kippur is the one day of the year that all streets are completely empty of any moving vehicles, whereas on a regular Shabbat, some still drive the streets (except in religious areas where they would risk being stoned). This has created an interesting and peculiarly

Israeli children's Yom Kippur custom. On this day, rather than spending the day fasting and praying with their parents in the synagogues, the children fill the streets with their bicycles and roller blades. It reminded me, with joy, of the scripture promising that one day

> **"the streets of the city** (Jerusalem) **would be filled with boys and girls playing in its streets!"**
> (Zechariah 8:5)

So, too, did the prophet Zechariah foresee the day that this solemn fast would one day be transformed into a joyous feast.

> **"The fasts of the fourth, fifth, seventh and tenth months will become joyful and glad occasions and happy festivals for Judah."**
> (Zechariah 8:19)

Biblical Background

As parents, we want our children to obey us on the first command. We don't want to have to give them an instruction over and over again. So when God repeats Himself several times, we know He must be serious about it! Such it is with Yom Kippur and his repeated instruction to afflict our souls and not to work on this day.

> **"And the Lord spoke to Moses, saying: 'Also the tenth day of this seventh month shall be the Day of Atonement. It shall be a holy convocation for you; you shall afflict your souls, and offer an offering made by fire to the Lord. And you shall <u>do no work</u> on that same day, for it is the Day of Atonement, to make atonement for you before the Lord your**

> God. For any person who is not afflicted in soul on that same day shall be cut off from his people. And any person who does any work on that same day, that person I will destroy from among his people. You shall **do no manner of work**; it shall be a statute forever throughout your generations in all your dwellings. It shall be to you a Sabbath of solemn rest, and you shall afflict your souls; on the ninth day of the month at evening, from evening to evening, you shall celebrate your Sabbath.'"
>
> (Leviticus 23:26-32)

> "This shall be a statute forever for you: In the seventh month, on the tenth day of the month, you shall afflict your souls, and do no work at all, whether a native of your own country or a stranger who dwells among you. For on that day the priest shall make atonement for you, to cleanse you, that you may be clean from all your sins before the Lord. It is a Sabbath of solemn rest for you, and you shall afflict your souls. It is a statute forever. And the priest, who is anointed and consecrated to minister as priest in his father's place, shall make atonement, and put on the linen clothes, the holy garments."
>
> (Leviticus 16:29-32)

Faith to Fear

The ten days between Yom Truah and Yom Kippur are called the ten days of fear (awe) (Yamim Noram'im). Whereas Yom Kippur had once been celebrated in confident anticipation of purification from sin, the Jewish people are not so confident today. They spend their time abstaining from all food and water (even toothpaste!), from sexual relations, wearing leather, or anointing with oil. Some even abstain from combing their hair. Many Jewish people weep and plead before the Lord instead of entering into His rest in remembrance of His compassion. Why? Because the sacrifice of the Cohen HaGadol (the High Priest) is no longer being performed on their behalf. No longer do the Jewish people have assurance of forgiveness of their sins.

Some hope to obtain pardon by substituting an animal like a rooster, chicken or fish. They swing it around their heads while reciting a prayer; *"This is my substitute, my vicarious offering, my atonement. This chicken/rooster will die so that I may obtain a long and pleasant life of peace."*

Most Jewish people in 'civilised' countries no longer swing the rooster over their heads, but instead substitute 'tzedakah' – charity money. They hold the coins in their hands and wave it around their heads, reciting the same prayer. This is very sad that, so desperate to know God's forgiveness, they would even offer a few coins. Many rabbis use this time to collect money for their yeshivot (schools of learning) and the synagogues usually campaign at this time for Israeli bonds, as the people hope that the giving of their charity would gain them favour in God's sight. Some recite this prayer and observe the custom, simply out of religious ritual, without any real understanding of the deep significance of the principle of atonement by blood.

> **"Neither their silver nor their gold shall be able to deliver them in the day of the Lord's wrath. But the whole land shall be devoured by the fire of His jealousy, for He will make speedy riddance of all those who dwell in the land."**
>
> (Zepheniah 1:18)

Fear to Faith

After I came to know Yeshua, I could no longer in good faith observe this family custom and I had to say, *"Yeshua is my substitute; He died in exchange for me; He died so that I could have life; He is my kapparah (atonement)."*

We who know Yeshua believe that no longer is an annual sacrifice necessary. He has made restitution for our sins once and for all. Money cannot make atonement for our sins. The price of a man's soul is too costly. (Psalm 49:6-9) Yeshua has freely redeemed us without money. He willingly paid the ransom at the cost of his own life. (John 10:11)

> **"You have sold yourselves for nothing, and you shall be redeemed without money."**
> (Isaiah 52:3)

What are We Saved From?

What are we saved from? When someone first told me that Jesus died for me to save me, I thought, *"Poor man, but I never asked Him to die for me."* I seriously did not understand why someone needed to die for me or that I needed to be saved from anything. Many Jewish people, even those like myself, raised in Orthodox, religious homes, do not receive a firm foundation in biblical principles of sin, sacrifice, and salvation.

Atonement

The Azazel

In the book of Leviticus, chapter 16 details the scriptural foundation of Yom Kippur – that an animal must be sacrificed to make atonement for our sins. One goat was slaughtered, and the other, the scapegoat, was sent into the wilderness to azazel, symbolically carrying the sins of the nation out of the midst of the people. Rabbinical tradition states that the cohen (Jewish priest) would tie a scarlet cloth to the horn of the goat for azazel and that when the sacrifice was fully accepted, the scarlet cloth became white. This symbolised God's gracious promise in Isaiah 1:18: **"Though your sins are like scarlet, they shall be white as snow."**

Tradition also adds that this miracle did not take place for forty years before the destruction of the temple.[1] Why? Because Yeshua was already sacrificed and the ritual of the azazel was no longer necessary nor accepted by God. The word azazel is used as a curse in Hebrew. It means 'go to Satan'. Yeshua became a curse for us, in order that we would no longer be under the curses of the kingdom of darkness. (Gal.3:13) He gave His life as the azazel, the scapegoat, for us. There is no greater love than this.

The Way of Salvation - Through the Blood of the Lamb

There is no difference between the way of salvation for a Jew or for a Gentile:

> **"There is no difference, for all have sinned and fall short of the glory of God. By God's grace, without**

---

1 Alfred Edersheim, *'The Temple'*, pg. 249

> earning it, all are granted the status of being considered righteous before Him, through the act redeeming us from our enslavement to sin that was accomplished by the Messiah Yeshua. God presented Him as a sacrifice of atonement (kapparah) through faith in his blood."
>
> (Romans 3:22-25)

In this way, Yeshua is the fulfilment of Yom Kippur. Why is the blood necessary? For atonement - to obtain forgivness of our sins.

> "For the life of a creature is in the blood, and I have given it to you to make atonement for yourselves on the altar; it is the blood that makes atonement for one's life."
>
> (Leviticus 17:11)

This is God's way, and who are we to question God? This is consistent with the faith of the Israelites with the blood of the lamb in Egypt. They applied the blood of the slain lamb to the sides and tops of the doorframes of their houses, according to God's instructions through Moses, so that the destruction of God would 'pass over' them.

> "The blood will be a sign for you on the houses where you are; and when I see the blood, I will pass-over you. No destructive plague will touch you when I strike Egypt... When the Lord goes through the land to strike down the Egyptians, He will see the blood on the top and sides of the doorframe and will pass over that doorway, and He will not permit the destroyer to enter your houses and strike you down."
>
> (Exodus 12:13, 23)

Yom Kippur Day of Atonement

This was a perfect foreshadowing of the Messiah. When John saw Yeshua coming towards him, he said,

> **"Look, the Lamb of God who takes away the sins of the world."**
>
> (John 1:29)

He entered Jerusalem on the 10th of Nissan, was inspected and assessed by the people for the required four days and found to be without blemish, and was then slain in order to fulfil the words of the prophets.

Yeshua the Suffering Servant of Isaiah 53

Yeshua willingly gave himself as a scapegoat for our sins.

> **"But He was pierced for our transgressions, He was crushed for our iniquities; the punishment that brought us peace was upon Him, and by His wounds we are healed…"**
>
> (Isaiah 53:5)

The *Cohen haGadol* the high priest laid the sins of the nation of Israel on the scapegoat *azazel* (Lev.16:21) So, too, did the Lord lay our sins upon Yeshua, the suffering servant.

> **The Lord has laid on Him the iniquity (sin) of us all.**
>
> (Isaiah 53:6)

No one took Yeshua's life from him. He gave it willingly for our sakes. (John10:18)

He was oppressed and afflicted, yet He did not open His mouth; He was led like a lamb to the slaughter... For He was cut off from the land of the living, for the transgression of My people He was stricken... for He bore the sin of many, and made intercession for the transgressors."

(Isaiah 53:7-12)

These words of the ancient Hebrew prophet, Isaiah, powerfully describe how Yeshua fulfilled Yom Kippur in sacrificing His own life to make atonement for our sins. Unfortunately, this reading is omitted from the yearly cycle of haftarah (prophetic) readings in the synagogues, effectively 'hiding' it from our own people. The parashah (portion of scripture) skips from Isaiah 52 to 54, so even if a Jewish person has faithfully attended services every Shabbat and read the Torah readings, they would have been denied access to the truth about Yeshua. Anti-missionaries claim that these scriptures refer, not to the Messiah, but to Israel. However, if we read closely, we can easily see that substituting Israel for Messiah does not work! Isaiah says that he was stricken for 'my people'. Who are Isaiah's people? Israel. How can Israel make atonement for Israel? Besides this, verse seven says that 'he was oppressed and afflicted, yet he did not open his mouth'. When Jewish people suffer, we usually hear loud complaints, myself included!

Even the ancient rabbis, prior to Yeshua's day, agreed that Isaiah 53 refers to the suffering and death of a personal Messiah for our sins. *"Our rabbis with one voice accept and affirm the opinion that the prophet (Isaiah) is here (ch.53) speaking of the Messiah."* [2]

Only later, in a reaction against Yeshua, did they deny these statements. But some rabbis are re-discovering these scriptural truths and coming to faith on their own through the Holy Spirit.

---

2 See R. Moses Alshech (16th century), *'Rabbinical Comments About the Messiah'*.

Our sins were symbolically transferred to the Messiah, who became our 'scapegoat'. But the blood of bulls and goats can never fully remove sin, only cover it for a time. A perfect, absolutely sinless one was required to pay the price for our rebellion and uncleanness. Only Yeshua the Messiah could fulfil this role. He willingly gave his life as the kapparah (atonement), the korban (sacrifice) for our sins.

> "He did not enter by means of the blood of goats and calves; but He entered the Most Holy Place once for all by His own blood, having obtained eternal redemption."
>
> (Hebrews 9:12)

The Arm of the Lord

God sent His own right arm to save us – not only the Jews but all of mankind.

> "The Lord will lay bare His *holy arm* in the sight of all the nations, and all the ends of the earth will see the salvation (yeshuah) of our God."
>
> (Isaiah 52:10)

We cannot think that by being a good person, or by giving our lives to charitable works, or in sacrifice for our children and grandchildren, that we have assurance of God's salvation. A blood sacrifice was always required to atone for our sins.

> "For the life of a creature is in the blood, and I have given it to you to make atonement for yourselves on the altar; it is the blood that makes atonement for one's life."
>
> (Leviticus 17:11)

This may seem strange to us, but this is the way of salvation given by God and who are we, the clay, to question the potter?

> **"For My thoughts are not your thoughts, neither are your ways My ways."**
>
> (Isiah 55:8)

God is so pure and so holy, that sin simply cannot dwell in His presence. Our sins sever our relationship with our God.

> **"Surely *the arm of the Lord* is not too short to save, nor his ear too dull to hear. But your iniquities have separated you from your God; your sins have hidden His face from you, so that He will not hear."**
>
> (Isaiah 59:1-2)

Yom Tru'ah and Yom Kippur may have been spent praying and fasting, but can we be sure that God has heard, or does God seem distant and silent? His desire is to draw near to each one of His children through the atonement of the sacrifice of His own arm, Yeshua HaMashiach (the Messiah) – His own arm.

> **"The Lord looked and was displeased that there was no justice. He saw that there was no one, he was appalled that there was no one to intervene; so His own arm worked salvation for Him... The Redeemer will come to Zion, to those in Jacob who repent of their sins."**
>
> (Isaiah 59:15, 16, 20)

Trying to have a relationship with God without the Messiah is like the high jump champion of the world attempting to reach the moon. He might be good, but he's not that good! All of us have sin in our lives, no matter how hard we try to be good people. God has made a way to overcome our faults and weaknesses. It is only the blood of Yeshua that covers us in righteousness so that we can stand before Him on the day of judgement.

> **"For He made Him (Jesus) who knew no sin to be sin for us, that we might become the rightesouness of God in Him."**
> (2 Corinthian 5:21)

The time has come, whether Jew or Gentile, to repent of our sins and accept the free gift of salvation that has already been poured out for us – the Lord's own blood spilled not upon the altar, but across the dusty ground. The temple has been destroyed. Animal sacrifices can no longer make the necessary atonement for our sins. After all the praying, and fasting and repenting, and giving of charity, and doing an abundance of good deeds, all one can hope for is an optimistic 'maybe' that God has forgiven. But when we, by faith, place the blood of Yeshua, the Lamb of God, over the door-frames of our heart, God will see the blood of the lamb and His wrath and destruction that is soon to fall upon this earth will 'pass over' us.

The Narrow Gate of Life

> "If anyone's name was not found written in the Book of Life, he was thrown into the lake of fire."
> (Revelation 20:15)

How can we know that our names are written in this Book of Life? Yeshua tells us to enter through the narrow gate to salvation.

> "For wide is the gate and broad is the road that leads to destruction, and many enter through it. But small is the gate and narrow the road that leads to life, and only a few find it."
>
> (Matthew 7:13-14)

According to Jewish tradition, on Yom Tru'ah, the gates are opened in heaven; God sits on the throne and examines the deeds of men which are all recorded in the Book of Life. These gates remain open during the ten 'Days of Awe' between Yom Tru'ah and Yom Kippur. This is the day, on which God makes His final judgements, and at sundown the gates are closed and judgement is sealed. The final service in the synagogue is called Neilah, and means closing of a gate.

Neilah

As the last lingering grains of sand filter through the hourglass of the Day of Atonement, there is no moment in the biblical calendar more solemn. As the shadow of night draws near, the chanting of the cantor reaches a heart-breaking intensity. It is the time of the closing of the gate. Judgement will be sealed. The word neilah in Hebrew means the locking of a gate. In ancient days, as long as the sun shone, the gates of the temple were kept open. All who wanted to could enter. But at night, the gates were locked. From then on, no one could enter or leave. This name was applied to the closing service of Yom Kippur. Through the Messiah, a narrow gate is opened to a new life – a living relationship with the God of the universe and a promise of eternal life with Him. And yet so few find the gate. They keep trying to enter through other ways that do not lead to life - through relationships, careers, position or wealth. The true gate of life stands open. The shofar is sounding. Our God is beckoning, pleading, weeping along with His people. Won't you go through that door before its too late? Will you enter the gate that leads to truth? Will you walk through the door of goodness – before the gate swings shut and is forever closed?

I believe we are in the final period of God's grace in which the gate is still open for any to walk through into eternal life, but this gate will soon shut. The Psalmist wrote prophetically,

> **"This is the gate (sha'ar in Hebrew) of the Lord through which the righteous may enter."**
> (Psalm 118:20)

What is this gate? Yeshua tells us He is the only gate to salvation:

> **"I tell you the truth, I am the gate for the sheep…I am the gate (sha'ar); whoever enters through Me will be saved. He will come in and go out, and find pasture."**
> (John 10:7-9)

There are not many paths to God; any other path is a dead end, a blind alley, a false way. (John 10:8) If we are truly his sheep we will hear his voice and not follow the voice a stranger by whatever name (Mohammed, Buddah, Krishna, Shiva etc.) Yeshua is the only way to the father.

> **"I am the way, the truth, and the life. No one comes to the Father except through Me"**
> (John 14:6)

My hope and prayer, is that all people, Jews and Gentiles, would turn to the Lord in sincere repentance. One day, perhaps soon, time will run out. The shofar will sound as an alarm and that fearful day of judgement will be upon us.

> "Blow the shofar in Zion; sound the alarm on My holy hill. Let all who live in the land tremble, for the day of the Lord is coming. It is close at hand – a day of darkness and gloom, a day of clouds and blackness…The day of the Lord is great and very terrible. Who can endure it?"
>
> (Joel 2:1-2, 11)

God does not desire or require empty ritual of us; He wants our hearts.

> "'Even now,' declares the Lord, 'Return to Me with all your heart, with fasting and weeping and mourning.' Rend your heart and not your garments. Return to the Lord your God, for He is gracious and compassionate, slow to anger and abounding in love, and He relents from sending calamity. Who knows? He may turn and have pity and leave behind a blessing."
>
> (Joel 2:12-14)

When the Messiah Comes

So many Jewish people say; *"When the Messiah comes ..."* this or that will happen. A Samaritan woman at a well said the same. She was rejected by many as a mixed race woman, not pure enough for some, as Jews would not associate with Samaritans. Many people today have been so rejected by 'religious' people in churches that they have rejected the Lord Himself. This woman was sexually immoral and a failure at relationships, already having been married to five men, and now living with another man who was not her husband. So many people today flit from one misguided relationship to another – looking for love in all the wrong places. And yet Yeshua chose to reveal himself to this messed up, mixed up woman.

> **"The woman said, 'I know that Messiah is coming. When He comes, He will explain everything to us.' Then Yeshua declared, 'I who speak to you am He.'"**
>
> (John 4:25-26)

Just as a hospital is not for the healthy, but for the sick, Yeshua did not come to save the righteous, but the sinners – like me, and probably like you too.

> **"Just as Moses lifted up the snake in the desert, so the Son of Man must be lifted up, that everyone who believes in Him may have eternal life... Whoever believes in the Son has eternal life, but whoever rejects the Son will not see life, for God's wrath remains on him."**
>
> (John 3:14-15, 36)

If you believe this is the truth, then walk through that narrow gate to start your new life with a prayer such as this:

> "God of Israel, of Abraham, Isaac, and Jacob, Creator of the universe, I repent before You and accept the sacrifice of Yeshua (Jesus) as atonement for all of my sins. I ask You to cleanse me from my past and to cover me with the blood of Yeshua, the Lamb of God, so that I will be saved and protected from the wrath of God. I thank You for Your gift of eternal life, and ask You to give me a new heart, and a new Spirit to guide me into living in a way pleasing to You. Amen."

Note: If you just prayed this prayer and would like to contact me, I would love to hear from you. Please write to the address on this book.

Born Again – The Mikvah

Praying this prayer and believing in your heart that Yeshua (Jesus) is the Messiah and atonement for our sins is a wonderful first step. But just as after a baby takes a first step and then keeps on stepping, so must we learn to 'walk' with the Lord. What good would it do a baby to take one step and then sit down on his toochus (yiddish for 'bottom') for the rest of his life? I'm going to be thrilled to see my youngest take his first step, I know. But I have every expectation that he will learn to walk and even run! Believing is not enough; it must be accompanied by action.

The Bible says that

> **"Faith by itself, if not accompanied by action is dead."**
>
> (James 2:17)

In the same way, simply saying this prayer, or re-committing our life to the Lord without any change in behaviour is fruitless. Now we need to begin a journey of finding out what pleases the Lord and what He hates. For this purpose, one needs to read His book (the Bible), study it, get together with other true Believers, and be discipled, just as Yeshua's followers were discipled. The next essential step is to be immersed in the waters of the mikvah (usually called Baptism).

> **"He who believes and is baptised will be saved."**
>
> (Mark 16:16)

It is a visible sign of repentence and a desire to turn back to God. Symbolically, we re-enter the watery womb and re-emerge as a new creation – born again. Yeshua said,

> **"unless one is born of water and the Spirit, he cannot enter the kingdom of God...You must be born again."**
>
> (John 3:5-7)

We must be baptised in water and in the Holy Spirit to have the power to live a Spirit-filled life. Many people in this day are choosing to be re-immersed and I believe it is a move of the Spirit and a sign of the Lord's soon coming return. Just as a Jewish bride will be immersed in the mikvah as a ritual purification in preparation for her wedding, believers are doing the same in preparation of the Bride for her soon coming Bridegroom, the Messiah.

What Must I Do to be Saved?

This is a crucial question that requires much soul searching. I don't believe it is as black and white as the mainstream Christian Church, which emphasizes salvation by grace alone, would make it out to be. When a Jewish man asked Yeshua this same question,

> **"Teacher, what good thing must I do to get eternal life?" the Messiah replied, "If you want to enter into life, keep the commandments."**
>
> (Matthew 19:16-17)

The man replied that he kept all the commandments that Yeshua specified, but there was still one thing lacking. He needed to sell his possessions and give to the poor. The young man went away very sad. Obviously Yeshua, who knows our hearts, discerned that money was an idol in this man's life. God must be number one; we may have no other gods besides Him. I am thankful that it is God and not I who is the judge of mankind. We need not concern ourselves with things too high and wonderful for us to comprehend. Our responsibility is to live our lives in righteousness and believe in the atonement He has provided through His Son, Yeshua, in order that we may stand before Him on the day of judgement.

The balance to this issue is that we must beware of self righteousness and realise our desperate need for a Saviour. It was the repentant sinner who, in humility, acknowledged his need of God's forgivness through mercy and grace alone who went home justified and right with God. In contrast, the Pharisee - boasting in his arrogance and pride trusted in his own righteousness. This man went home unforgiven and separated from God, no matter how holy he considered himself in his own eyes. Yeshua called men such as these hypocrites,

> **"like whitewashed tombs which indeed appear beautiful outwardly, but inside are full of dead men's bones and all uncleanness."**
>
> (Matthew 23:27)

For God does not look on the outward appearance, but upon our hearts. Men may be fooled by outward appearances of righteousness but God sees through our hypocrisy.

> **"Even so you also outwardly appear righteous to men, but inside you are full of hypocrisy and lawlessness."**
>
> (Matthew 23:28)

Hypocrites such as these put themselvves in danger of the

condemnation of hell.

On the other hand... Have you seen that wonderful movie, Fidler on the Roof? The main character, a Jewish man named Tevia, keeps looking at the situations in his life from various angles, saying, "On the other hand...on the other hand..." This is the situation we have here. The issue of salvation is complex. Many scriptures promise us salvation by faith alone.

> **"For God so loved the world that whoever believes on Him shall not perish but have eternal life."**
> (John 3:16)

However, other less emphasized scriptures warn us that we will be judged and even our eternal fate decided on the basis of what we have done in our lives, both good and bad.

> **"Do not be amazed at this, for a time is coming when all who are in their graves will hear His voice and come out – those who have done good will rise to live, and those who have done evil will rise to be condemned."**
> (John 5:28-29)

We truly need to come to a balance of faith and works. The people of Israel, when warned of impending judgment, turned to the Prophet Micah with the question,

> **"What does God really require of us?"**
> (Micah 6:8)

Many of us, at times, struggle with this question as well – what is it that God really wants from us? Some who believe in the sacrifice of Yeshua consider this enough – that their behavior makes no difference to God whatsoever. *"I'm saved by the blood of Jesus. Period. End of story."* Yes, we need to always depend upon the grace of God demonstrated in the sacrifice of His Son, Yeshua, to atone for our sins, but there is more that God requires of us than this faith. Jewish people are often criticized for their emphasis on 'works' – doing good deeds or mitzvot in order to please God. Christians are often criticized for their attitude that their 'deeds' don't count, and that they can therefore sin and not be penalized. We must, however, mature into a balance of faith and deeds that harmonize one with another.

> **"It has been told to you, Adam (man), what is good, and what the Lord requires of you; only to do justly, and to love mercy, and to walk humbly with thy God."**
>
> (Micah 6:8)

In Hebrew, mercy is translated as 'chessed', meaning 'kindness to the lowly, needy and miserable, as shown in all charitable acts, especially such as go with personal service.' Even the New Testament proclaims that

> **"faith without works is dead."**
>
> (James 2:17)

What is true religion?

> **"Religion that God our Father accepts as pure and faultless is this: to look after orphans and widows in their distress and to keep oneself from being polluted by the world."**
>
> (James 1:27)

Our task on Yom Kippur then, is not simply to deny ourselves food and drink and sit in a hot, stuffy shule (synagogue) all day, listening to the chazzan (cantor) chant all the prayers. It is to enter into a new life of righteousness. This is the fast that God calls for.

True Fasting

On Yom Kippur, we are commanded to fast and pray – to seek the Lord's mercy because of our sins. And yet, Isaiah tells us what the Lord considers true fasting. It is not putting on a long face and sitting in the synagogue (or church) all day, dressed in our finest clothes, complaining about how hungry we are. It is not ending the fast with tea and honey cake and then carrying on with our lives just as they were the days and years before we fasted. Simply fasting will not guarantee the attention of God. This is what the Lord says,

> **"You cannot fast as you do today and expect your voice to be heard on high. Is this the kind of fast I have chosen, only a day for a man to humble himself?... Is not this the kind of fasting I have chosen: to loose the chains of injustice and untie the cords of the yoke, to set the oppressed free and break every yoke? Is it not to share your food with the hungry and to provide the poor wanderer with shelter – when you see the naked, to clothe him, and not to turn away from your own flesh and blood?"**
> (Isaiah 58:4-7)

I remember my Baba, my old grandmother, before she died, standing at the doorway with her apron on, handing out dollar bills to the poverty-stricken, Native children that came to her home, knowing she would always give to the needy. I knew that we would usually have an extra guest for lunch or dinner at our table after synagogue, as my Mother would scan the congregation, seeking the stranger who might need a meal and friendly fellowship. I thank God for the heritage of a family who modelled justice, charity and righteousness.

What does God promise as a reward for serving Him in this way?

> "**Then your light will break forth like the dawn, and your healing will quickly appear; then your righteousness will go before you, and the glory of the Lord will be your rear guard. Then you will call, and the Lord will answer; you will cry for help, and He will say: 'Here I am.'"**
>
> (Isaiah 58:8-9)

Do we need help, guidance, healing, and strength from the Lord? Let us stop pointing fingers and criticizing everything that is wrong with others (or ourselves); instead, we must set out to find someone worse off than ourselves and do something to help them.

> "**If you do away with the yoke of oppression, with the pointing finger and malicious talk, and if you spend yourselves in behalf of the hungry and satisfy the needs of the oppressed, then your light will rise in the darkness, and your night will become like the noonday. The Lord will guide you always; He will satisfy your needs in a sun-scorched land and will strengthen your frame. You will be like a well-watered garden like a spring whose waters never fail.**"
>
> (Isaiah 58:9-11)

The following is a devotional, which expresses this sentiment.[3]

The Protester and the Prophet

>I was hungry
>and you formed a humanities club
>and discussed my hunger.
>Thank you.
>
>I was imprisoned
>and you crept off quietly
>to your chapel in the cellar
>and prayed for my release.
>
>I was naked
>and in your mind
>you debated the morality
>of my appearance.
>
>I was sick
>and you thanked God
>for your good health.
>
>I was homeless
>and you preached to me
>of the spiritual shelter
>of the love of God.
>
>I was lonely
>and you left me alone
>to pray for me.

---

3   From the High Holy Day supplement in an Orthodox Jewish synagogue.

You seem so holy;
so close to God.
But I'm still very hungry
and lonely
and cold …

> **"Is not this the fast that I have chosen?**
> **To loose the fetters of wickedness,**
> **To undo the bonds of the yoke,**
> **And to let the oppressed go free.**
> **And that ye break every yoke?"**
>
> (Isaiah 58:5-6)

CHAPTER THREE

SUKKOT – FEAST OF TABERNACLES / BOOTHS

Z'man Simchateinu - Season of Our Joy

The Feast of Sukkot completes the cycle of the Fall Feasts for the seventh month of the biblical calendar. We have passed through the seasons of repentance and mourning; now is the time to rejoice.

> "Weeping may remain for a night, but joy cometh in the morning."
>
> (Psalm 30:5)

For a moment in an eternity of time, God may have demonstrated His wrath, but we may now rejoice in the prophetic awareness that He will once again 'pass over' us and we will have been saved. We rejoice that our names are written in the Book of Life in heaven. (Luke 10:20) We celebrate the life of peace and joy that we have in relationship with Him through Yeshua HaMashiach. Therefore, we call Sukkot the time (season) of our joy.

> "To everything there is a season. A time for every purpose under heaven:..a time to weep and a time to laugh (the Hebrew word לשחוק Lesachek means also to play); a time to mourn, and a time to dance."
>
> (Ecclesiastes 3:1, 4)

Sukkot is the time to rejoice, to laugh, to play and to dance.

The following is an e-mail communication that we sent out from Jerusalem during Sukkot 2000:

Shmini Atzeret – Last Day of the Feast

Shalom from Jerusalem:

Today is Shmini Atzeret, the eighth day, the last day of the Feast of Sukkot (Tabernacles/Booths). The people of Israel, despite the imminent danger of war and the continuing tragedies occurring throughout the country, gathered to rejoice before the Lord as commanded. Shmuel, Liat (our children) and I made a tour of a couple of the neighborhood synagogues and joined in the singing and dancing. I raise my voice along with my people to cry out to the Lord,

> "Ana Adonai" (Answer, Lord),
> "Hoshiana, Adonai" (Save us, Lord).

We look forward to the time when the promises of God for Israel will become a reality with the coming of the Messiah Yeshua and we shall weep no more.

> **"For the people shall dwell in Zion at Jerusalem. You shall weep no more. He will be very gracious to you at the sound of your cry. When He hears it, He will answer you."**
>
> (Isaiah 30:19)

Of course the old Baba's in the shule (synagogue) love Shmuel and Liatty and made sure they each got their own bag of candies in honor of the chag (holiday), even if this meant hollering down to the men below until they finally brought up a bag for them.

Liat has learned to clap her hands just in time for the occasion and loves clapping to the music. She has also discovered snails in Israel. She is now standing and proud of it!

Timothy (Shmuel), I notice, is beginning to use Hebrew as his language of play when he is by himself, playing with cars or marbles (as little boys do). Occasionally, he has to substitute a word due to his still limited vocabulary. The rabbit (arnevet) needed to be a mouse (achbar) for this purpose, but I think we're making progress! The challenge may be for him to remember his English, but I read English books to him every night that my sisters brought us when visiting Israel. Todah rabah!!

During the week, we attended a very special ceremony at the Kotel (Western Wall). The roads were blocked off, but we got in through Zion gate and joined thousands and thousands of worshippers, dancing, singing, and rejoicing before the Lord. The ceremony is called, '**Simchat Beit Ha-shoeva**' (Rejoicing of the House of Drawing Water). It originates in a custom which began during the second temple period, in which the cohen (priest) would take a pitcher down to the Pool of Shiloach (Siloam) and fill it with water, walk back to the temple and pour it out upon the altar. As the cohen would walk, a procession would follow him, rejoicing, dancing, and singing the Hallel (praise) Psalms.

You would not believe the exuberance and wild abandon with which both the men and women (segregated, of course) were dancing. A Chassidic musician was playing live, joyful music, broadcast throughout the Kotel area, about the coming of the Messiah and the re-building of the temple. I began to think about the denominational churches we have been in that forbid dancing (although most loosened up a bit when we were through with them!). I was imagining that if they could see this scene, they would be appalled, and probably consider it pagan and heathen. But what is actually heathen? We see in many scriptures that praising and worshipping the Lord with dancing, musical instruments, and singing is not only allowed by God, but even commanded.

> **"Praise Him with the sound of the shofar. Praise Him with the lute and harp. Praise Him with the timbrel and dance."**
>
> (Psalm 150:3-4)

King David also danced like a fool before the Lord and we would do well to take note of the fate of his wife, Michal, who despised him for this wild dancing. She remained barren for the rest of her life. (2 Sam. 6:14-23) So, I believe, do churches remain dry and barren as far as the Spirit of God, who despise those who praise the Lord with dance. Let's bring the biblical practice of dance back into the churches and speak the truth to those who forbid this gift.

It wasn't until we returned home from the celebration at the Kotel and I checked in Barney Kasdan's book, God's Appointed Times, that I pieced everything together. This ceremony of the rejoicing of the drawing of the water, celebrates not only the hope of winter rains in Israel, but also symbolizes the future Messianic Redemption at which time the Spirit of God, symbolized by the water, is poured out upon this nation. It is possible, if not likely, that this was the setting when Yeshua stood up and proclaimed Himself to be the fulfillment of this ceremony:

> "On the last day, that great day of the feast, Yeshua stood and cried out, saying, 'If anyone thirst, let him come to Me and drink. He who believes in Me, as the Scripture has said, out of his heart will flow rivers of living water."
>
> (John 7:37-38)

Courtney (our older daughter) affirmed that a compelling Spirit of joy seemed to come upon her as she joined the women in dancing. But we know that even this joy cannot compare to the joy that we will one day experience with the fulfillment of the Feast of Sukkot, when Yeshua returns to rule and reign over all the nations with perfect justice and righteousness from his capital city, Jerusalem!

We know that when Yeshua returns, it will be to defend Israel and Jerusalem and to destroy the nations that come against her.

> "In that day the Lord will defend the inhabitants of Jerusalem; the one who is feeble among them in that day shall be like David, and the house of David shall be like God, like the angel of the Lord before them. It shall be in that day that I will seek to destroy all the nations that come against Jerusalem."
>
> (Zechariah 12:8-9)

I hope this message encourages you today.
Chag Sameach (Happy Holidays) from Jerusalem.

Love Hannah

Scriptural Background to Sukkot

God commanded His people to celebrate Sukkot, to meet on the first and last day, to wave leafy branches before the Lord in thanksgiving and to live in temporary shelters for seven days - like a glorified week of community camping.

> "Then the Lord spoke to Moses, saying, 'Speak to the children of Israel, saying: 'The fifteenth day of this seventh month shall be the Feast of Tabernacles for seven days to the Lord. On the first day there shall be a holy convocation. You shall do no customary work on it. For seven days you shall offer an offering made by fire to the Lord. On the eighth day you shall have a holy convocation, and you shall offer an offering made by fire to the Lord. It is a sacred assembly, and you shall do no customary work on it. ..
>
> And you shall take for yourselves on the first day the fruit of beautiful trees, branches of palm trees, the boughs of leafy trees, and willows of the brook; and you shall rejoice before the Lord your God for seven days. You shall keep it as a feast to the Lord for seven days in the year. It shall be a statute forever in your generations.
>
> You shall celebrate it in the seventh month. You shall dwell in booths for seven days. All who are native Israelites shall dwell in booths, that your generations may know that I made the children of Israel dwell in booths when I brought them out of the land of Egypt: I am the Lord your God.' So Moses declared to the children of Israel the feasts of the Lord."
>
> (Leviticus 23:33-44)

Sukkot - Feast of Tabernacles / Booths 89

The Real Thanksgiving

Most North Americans celebrate Thanksgiving weekend with a festive meal of turkey (with stuffing of course!) mashed potatoes with gravy and pumpkin pie with whipping cream. One of my cravings in Israel was for pumpkin pie, since the canned filling has not yet reached these Middle Eastern grocery shelves. A dear sister in the Lord, who heard of this, actually brought me a freshly baked pumpkin pie from Canada this year. People can be very special. We have much to be grateful for. We often take so much for granted and forget to thank God for the very beds we sleep in, the roof over our heads, running water in the bathroom (which runs warm when the sun's out), an indoor toilet. At least most in North America enjoy these conveniences and blessings. We have one another – and most of all – we have a Good Shepherd who always watches over us and cares for us in whatever situation we find ourselves.

A delicious Thanksgiving dinner can be a perfect opportunity to bring these things to mind and to thank God for them. But how many Christians realize that the *real* Thanksgiving (biblically speaking) is Sukkot. The pilgrims knew about this feast and 'adapted' it to the modern day Thanksgiving. How many other customs have been changed from the biblical command by man's initiative?

This feast celebrates the latter day harvest and prophesies the latter day harvest of souls. Yeshua often spoke in parables about crops and harvests to a primarily agricultural people.

> **"When He saw the crowds, He had compassion on them, because they were harassed and helpless, like sheep without a shepherd. Then He said to His disciples, 'The harvest is plentiful but the workers are few. Ask the Lord of the harvest, therefore, to send out workers into His harvest field."**
>
> (Matthew 9:36-38)

Yehovah is Lord of the harvest. Sukkot may very well be His appointed time to bring in a great harvest of souls at the end of the age.

The Sukkah (Tabernacle)

The sukkah is a booth or dwelling that the children of Israel are commanded to build and live in for the entire week of Sukkot, especially in the Land of Israel. During this feast of seven days, the people lived, as commanded, in temporary shelters to commemorate God's miraculous provisions for His people, even while wandering for forty years in a desert wilderness. We celebrate His protective care over us at all times. During harvest time in Israel, the land would be dotted with sukkot. It was and is, in essence, a biblically mandated, week-long camping holiday. What fun if we would and could only observe this commandment.

Unfortunately, in Israel today, most people simply build a token sukkah on their balcony or in the back yard (if they are fortunate enough to have one) and eat some meals or fellowship in the sukkah. By living in a temporary dwelling for a week, we remember that this earth is not our true home, but that we are only strangers and aliens here. Our true citizenship is in heaven.

> **"For our citizenship is in heaven, from which we also eagerly wait for the Savior, the Lord Jesus ישוע (Yeshua)[1] the Messiah."**
>
> (Philippians 3:20)

---

1 Yeshua - Hebrew name of Jesus.

Hiding in God's Sukkah

The original Hebrew of Psalm 27 uses 'Sukkot' terminology to describe God's protection over His people.

> "For in the day of trouble, He will keep me safe in His sukkah."
>
> (Psalm 27:5)

I believe that during this time of the pouring out of God's final destruction upon the earth, God will draw His people up into the protective covering of His heavenly dwelling, His mansion, to hide us from His wrath. This must occur at His coming, not before. The dead will be resurrected and the people of the earth judged. The prophet Isaiah foresaw the resurrection and God's 'calling up' of His people.'

> "But your dead will live;
> their bodies will rise.
> You who dwell in the dust,
> wake up and shout for joy.
> Your dew is like the dew of the morning;
> The earth will give birth to her dead.
> Go, my people, enter your rooms
> And shut the doors behind you;
> Hide yourselves for a little while
> Until His wrath has passed by,
> See, the Lord is coming out of His dwelling
> to punish the people of the earth for their sins."
>
> (Isaiah 26:19-21)

Where are these rooms that God calls His people to hide in behind shut doors? Yeshua tells us not to let our hearts be troubled, but to trust in God, and also in Him.

> "In My Father's house are many rooms; if it were not so, I would have told you. I am going there to prepare a place for you. And if I go and prepare a place for you, I will come back and take you to be with Me that you also may be where I am...I am the way and the truth and the life. No one comes to the Father except through Me."
>
> (John 14:1-6)

In beautiful imagery of Hebraic wedding customs, Yeshua – as the bridegroom – is gone away to prepare a place for His bride in His father's house, as was the custom. The bride does not know exactly when her bridegroom will come to fetch her, but she keeps herself ready and when the time draws near for his return, she keeps her oil lamps lit in case he comes in the night. What a profound picture of the coming of the Bridegroom for His bride, like a 'thief in the night' and the bride making herself ready. No matter what we go through in the future, we may bring peace to our hearts with the knowledge that Yeshua has gone to prepare a place for those who are His, and that we will have a hiding place there from His wrath.

The Prophetic Significance of Sukkot

The seventh and final shofar signals the last plague poured out upon the earth. Judgement will have been completed and the Messianic Age will begin. At this time,

> "the kingdom of the world has become the kingdom of our Lord and of His Messiah, and He will reign for ever and ever."
>
> (Revelation 11:15)

A Jew Takes Over the World

Finally, a Jew will make all the anti-Semites worst fears come true – a Jew will take over the world! The prophet Isaiah foretold that one day, a Jewish virgin would give birth to a child who would be עמנו אל "**Immanu-El** (God with us)."(Is. 7:14) This young, Jewish woman's name was Miryam. This child born to her, a son, would one day carry the government of the world and the very name of God upon His shoulders. He would be called, "פלא יועץ (Pele Yoetz) **Wonderful Counsellor,** אל גבור (El Gibor) **Mighty God,** אבי עד (Avi Ad) **Everlasting Father,** שר שלום (Sar Shalom) **Prince of Peace.**" His government would be eternal and He would reign on David's throne in justice and righteousness forever, fulfilling the words of the Hebrew prophets. (Is. 9:6-7)

> "Once for all, I have sworn by My holiness – and I will not lie to David – that his line will continue forever and his throne endure before Me like the sun."
>
> (Psalm 89:35-36)

God is not a man that He could lie. He fulfilled His promise in Yeshua HaMashiach. The angel Gabriel said to Miryam,

> "You will be with child and give birth to a Son, and you are to give Him the name Yeshua. He will be great and will be called the Son of the Most High. The Lord God will give Him the throne of His father David, and He will reign over the house of Jacob forever; His kingdom will never end."
>
> (Luke 1:31-33)

Sukkot/Tabernacles will one day be the time when all things are restored according to the prophetic word of God. It will be the time when the Lord Yeshua takes His throne and the Messiah reigns over the earth forever. Immanuel, God With Us, finally dwells (or tabernacles) with His people on earth.

> **"Now the dwelling (tabernacle or sukkah) of God is with men, and He will live with them and be their God. He will wipe every tear from their eyes. There will be no more death or mourning or crying or pain, for the old order of things has passed away."**
> (Revelation 21:3-4)

What a wonderful time to look forward to – the fulfilment of the seventh day Sabbath – perfect rest and peace for God's people.

Tabernacles – Yeshua's Birthday

Most Christians celebrate December 25th as the birthday of Jesus, calling it Christmas. Many are now discovering, and Christian scholars have long known that December 25th is probably not the birthday of Yeshua the Messiah. It is much more likely, from both a scholarly and prophetic perspective, to be Sukkot. Not only is the date December 25th a falsehood, but it also originates from a pagan day celebrating, not the Son of God, but the son of a heathen, pagan god who was supposedly killed and resurrected. Satan always tries to produce counterfeits to biblical truth. This feast, characterized by drunkenness and orgies, occurred on the date of the winter solstice and was called the Feast of Saturnalia. Is it any wonder that, despite Christians' best efforts to keep Jesus as 'the reason for the season', Christmas has become in some respects a commercialized, drunken farce, celebrated by the world?

Sukkot - Feast of Tabernacles / Booths

Most scholars agree that Jesus was most likely born in the fall, and since He has fulfilled the other feasts at God's appointed times, would it not make sense that Immanuel, 'God With Us' would be born and come to dwell (or tabernacle) with us on the Feast of Tabernacles? Sukkot is, therefore, a wonderful feast to celebrate together with the Jewish people for the added reason that we may rejoice that our Saviour was born at this festival time. Perhaps in each sukkah (temporary hut or tabernacle), a little baby in a cradle could occupy the corner to remind us of this wonderful event. The nativity scene in a sukkah? Well – it would be sure to draw some questions and open the door to share about a child who was born to a Jewish virgin named Miryam.

> **"Therefore the Lord Himself will give you a sign. Behold, the virgin shall conceive and bear a Son, and shall call His name Immanuel."**
>
> (Isaiah 7:14)

The Son given to us is called Wonderful Counsellor (Pele Yoetz), Mighty God (El Gibor), Everlasting Father (Aviad), and Prince of Peace (Sar Shalom). (Is. 9:6) This is Mashiach Ben David – the Messiah, Son of David.

John 1:14 tells us that the **"...word became flesh and dwelt among us."**

Although this feast was partially fulfilled with the birth of the Lord, it will reach its fullness when the Lord returns to earth to rule and reign as King Messiah from Jerusalem.

> **"Now the dwelling (sukkah) of God is with men, and He will live with them. They will be His people, and God Himself will be with them and be their God."**
>
> (Revelation 21:3)

The First Feast of the Millennium

Festival of the Nations

If we are seeking biblical evidence that the Feasts of the Lord are not abolished and that they are for all the people of God, Jew and Gentile, we need look no further than Sukkot. In fact, the Lord seems to feel so strongly about all His redeemed people celebrating His feast, that in the millennium, He curses any nation that refuses to come to Jerusalem to celebrate the Feast of Tabernacles.

> **"Then the survivors from all the nations that have attacked Jerusalem will go up year after year to worship the King, the Lord Almighty, and to celebrate the Feast of Tabernacles... The Lord will bring on them the plague He inflicts on the nations that do not go up to celebrate the Feast of Tabernacles. This will be the punishment of Egypt and the punishment of all the nations that do not go up to celebrate the Feast of Tabernacles."**
>
> (Zechariah 14:16-19)

For those who know nothing about this feast (or the other Feasts of the Lord); perhaps this would be a wonderful time to learn.

CHAPTER FOUR

THE SHELTER OF HIS WINGS

A Devotional for Sukkot – The Feast of Tabernacles

> "Be merciful to me, O God, be merciful to me! For my soul trusts in You; and in the shadow of Your wings I will make my refuge, until these calamities have passed by."
>
> (Psalm 57:1)

The morning started well enough. Driving to congregation went smoothly - the family even on time this morning, which was unusual, but a welcome relief from the frustration of our chronic tardiness. The sun was shining and the kids noticed that Mom was smiling; the world seemed a safe and happy place. I looked forward to serving in the nursery that morning and then attending a picnic after the service. Being the ever dutiful, devoted, and DYNAMO MOTHER, that I am this morning, I pop in our 'Drive Time Devotion' cassette tape into the player. "Might as well get a little of the Word hidden in our hearts this morning as we drive", I thought. The Devotion is short but sweet. It centers on courage – the knowledge that God is always with us so we don't need to fear. Specifically, the memory verse was from Deuteronomy 31:6:

"Be strong and of good courage, do not fear nor be afraid of them; for the Lord your God, He is the One who goes

with you. He will not leave you nor forsake you." I love this particular verse because it was the one that brought me to faith in Jesus (Yeshua).

For some reason, my son, Timothy, really picked up on this verse. He kept repeating it over and over (and over) again. No way was I ever going to forget this one! Recently I had bought him his very own first music CD to go in the portable CD player that Grandpa bought him for his 11th birthday. Timothy's key birth scripture is from the book of Timothy,

> **"God has not given us a spirit of fear, but of power and love and a sound mind."**
>
> (2 Timothy 1:7)

Sometimes God gives us a Word in advance to prepare us from something that is ahead. He knows we will need this word hidden in our heart in order to get through something in victory. And so I strengthened myself with this word of encouragement and breezed through my nursery duty.

After service, I drove to the park for the scheduled couples' ministry picnic. I happened to be alone with the children since my husband worked nights and needed to sleep in the mornings. I usually brought him the tape of the sermon to listen to later. Our plan was to meet at the picnic later. A twinge told me to give my husband a call but I ignored it. Not usually a good idea to ignore those little twinges. After enjoying the food, fun and fellowship of the picnic, I became irritated that my husband had not shown up. I noticed, offhand, that it had started to rain. No matter, our group was eating under the park's open picnic shelter. Finally I asked Vicki if I could use her cell phone to call my delinquent husband. "Which park?", he asked. "Sure, flimsy excuse," I think to myself (is that bitterness rearing its ugly head?). I give him the name of the park and he says he will try to be there. By this time, I notice that the rain was coming down really hard. "Boy, we're going to get soaked," I realized. Soon, the downpour turned into a solid sheet of water. It was as if the heavens had opened and Someone up there was pouring tons of water from some gigantic bucket. If not for the promise of the rainbow that God made to Noah that He would never flood the earth again, I would have been genuinely concerned. As if the torrential rain was not enough, it quickly turned into hail. First tiny granules of hail; then small pebbles and finally, hail hammered down upon the earth the size of marbles and larger. A strong wind kicked up as well, driving the hail into the shelter which left us open and vulnerable on all sides. I began to feel scared.

Vicki to the rescue again. She and her husband Robert put up a tarp on one end of the shelter to keep out most of the rain, wind and hail. Then they pulled out a huge comforter and two big pillows which we laid on the bench of the picnic table for Liat and Kaillee, my four year old daughter and her five year old friend. We covered them up completely so that the hail would not sting their faces. Rather than crying and feeling fear, they thought this was one big, fun adventure. Vicki and Robert's parents, visiting from Ontario, kept the girls covered and supplied with cheezies. We lay the baby on a blanket on another bench and he mercifully went to sleep for the duration of the storm. Someone built a fire in the hearth of the shelter to keep us warm. People who had been caught outside in the hail began to run inside to find shelter along with our fellowship group and warm up by the fire. People shared their coats and jackets with those who had none. There was a beautiful spirit of camaraderie under the shelter.

The cell phone rang. It was my husband David. "I can't get to you!", he shouted over the roar of the storm. The Police have blocked the road down to the park. They say you'll be stranded down there for hours. The freeway is completely flooded. Some of the roads are collapsing. Firefighters and emergency vehicles are trying to rescue people out of their cars and get them to safety." I fought a feeling of panic as he went on, "…and they've issued a tornado warning. Stay where you are!" I started to scream, "What do you mean you can't reach me? Tell the police that your wife and kids are down here and you have to drive down." "No way, they're not letting anyone down", he answered. Even if I could get out, the freeway route, which was the only access to my home was completely impassable. Tears came to my eyes.

It was then that I remembered God's word to me in the morning and I felt a sense of comfort and peace flooding my troubled emotions, **"Be strong and of good courage. Do not fear. I am with you."** I knew with all of my heart that God was with us and would help us. I saw how He had provided for everything we needed in the storm. I began to sing praises to my God and my King. "The Lord is my light and my salvation; I will trust and will not be afraid, for the Lord my God is my strength and my song, He also has become my salvation, Lah, lah, lah, lah....." I don't think anyone could hear me over the noise of the storm, but I know my God could hear. I went on, singing and singing, "You are my hiding place; you always fill my mouth with songs of deliverance; whenever I am afraid I will trust in You, I will trust in You; let the weak say I am strong in the strength of the Lord...." And finally, I sang, "O protector of my soul, you will stand against the foe. In the dark You'll be a light for me, O protector of my soul. You who created the ends of the earth; guided me unto Your throne. Offered your healing hand to me; mercifully made me Your own. O Protector of my soul..." I sang God's lullabies to my soul and was at peace in the midst of the storm, hidden under a secure shelter.

Eventually the rain and hail let up and I managed to drive to my parents' home, even though much of the road was flooded. Here, David and I were reunited and we embraced in relief that all of us were safe. Pictures in the newspaper the next day showed the devastation of this freak storm, but I had learned some important spiritual lessons through the experience.

First of all, I had (perhaps foolishly) prayed a day earlier for a wake up and shake up call. This was intended for my husband, who seemed content (in my eyes) to continue a path that I didn't feel was the will of God for our lives. But I knew that this storm was a wake up and shake up, not just for David alone but for us all. We know that God has promised He will judge the earth. Many prophets have been predicting that this time is soon.

> **"Surely there is a reward for the righteous; surely He is God who judges in the earth."**
> (Psalm 58:11)

We know that God will not turn a blind eye forever to the immorality, bloodshed, violence, injustice, and witchcraft that is taking over the earth in our day. He is a God of love, but also a God of justice. "Vengeance is Mine," says the Lord. Just as in the days of Noah, Yeshua (Jesus) warned us, people will carry on with their daily lives; business as usual, eating, working, shopping, getting married, parties, getting up, going to sleep, getting up, going to sleep, without a clue as to the judgment that would soon be upon them – until Noah entered the ark – and the flood destroyed them all.

> **"Therefore you also be ready, for the Son of Man is coming at an hour you do not expect."**
> (Matthew 25:36-44)

I looked at my husband and he looked at me and the same words were upon our lips, "We're not ready." We are not ready to enter into the terrible end-time tribulation period that is prophesied to come upon the earth. Very recently, someone sent us a tape called, Ten Tests in the Wilderness. The basic idea on the tape is that we will go through the same tests during the tribulation that the Israelites went through in the wilderness after their exit from Egypt. Through the example of their failures and resulting death in the wilderness, we can determine not to repeat their mistakes, but to be overcomers and, after we have suffered awhile, enter into the Kingdom of God, the true Promised Land.

> "Moreover, brethren, I do not want you to be unaware that all our fathers were under the cloud, all passed through the sea, all were immersed into Moses in the cloud and in the sea, all ate the same spiritual food, and all drank the same spiritual drink. For they drank of that spiritual Rock that followed them, and that Rock was Messiah. But with most of them God was not well pleased, for their bodies were scattered in the wilderness.
>
> <u>Now these things became our examples</u>, to the intent that we should not lust after evil things as they also lusted...Now <u>all these things happened to them as examples</u>, and <u>they were written for our admonition, upon whom the end of the ages have come.</u>"
>
> (1Corinthians 10:1-11)

These words were written for the generation that would face the end times, upon whom the end of the ages would come. Many believe that this generation will face that challenge. Technology today is racing ahead with innovations that will make end time prophecy fulfillment a piece of cake. Once again, the building of a tower of Babel is well underway – the unity of the New World Order – and nothing that their minds conceive of will be impossible for them. The ten tests that the Israelites went through have become examples to us, written for our admonition, so that we may not fail the tests.

The Mark Of The Beast

This is no airy fairy spiritual message about the end times. Living in Israel afforded us a 'test-run' – it foreshadowed many of the difficulties we may face. This message contains practical advice for ways that we must prepare to survive the tribulation. We know that no one will be able to buy or sell anything without taking the mark of the beast, whose number is 666.

> "**He causes all, both small and great, rich and poor, free and salve, to receive a mark on their right hand or on their foreheads, and that no one may buy or sell except one who has the mark or the name of the beast, or the number of his name...His number is 666.**"
> (Revelation 13:16-17)

For now, we use debit cards to buy or sell and may still use cash, checks, or credit cards. When I go to the grocery store, the scanner reads my personal information off my card and the clerk always says, "Have a good day, Mrs. Nesher", as if she knows me personally (which she doesn't). But the day may soon be upon us, especially if hit by another terrorist attack, when we may be forced into a cashless society where each person's identity number and personal information is implanted by a tiny microchip into their right hand or forehead. The ramifications of this are staggering. Even passports may be encoded in these microchips, causing it to become impossible for us to leave the country. Now the U.S. government is planning to take over the screening of people who board their aircrafts at the airports, hooking up their computers with a central database. If global anti-Semitism breaks out, as it did nationally in pre-WWII Nazi Germany, the Jewish people (and those who stand with them) may be unable to flee the country.

Because of our faith in Yeshua (Jesus), the government of Israel persecuted us by refusing to release our identity cards for a period of time. This meant that many things important to carry on with daily life were difficult and inconvenient. Until we received this identity card, we could not obtain health care benefits, nor the assistance and financial incentives given to new immigrants. I had a miscarriage and we could not afford medical care. We could not open a bank account or even mail a parcel without this crucial identity number. Everything we wanted to do in the country seemed to depend upon possessing this crucial number called a teudat zehut. So too, will the people of God who refuse to take the mark find many things they did previously now difficult if not impossible. But the Lord supernaturally provided during this time for all of our needs – food, clothing and shelter. We will need absolute trust in the Lord to sustain us and provide our needs rather than expect any help from government, educational or medical institutions.

Anyone who takes the mark of the Beast will doom themselves to eternal damnation and torment.

> **"If anyone worships the beast and his image, and receives his mark on his forehead or on his hand, he himself shall also drink of the wine of the wrath of God, which is poured out full strength into the cup of His indignation. He shall be tormented with fire and brimstone in the presence of the holy angels and in the presence of the Lamb. And the smoke of their torment ascends forever and ever; and they have no rest day or night, who worship the beast and his image, and whoever receives the mark of his name."**
> (Revelation 14:9-11)

How many young people know this information? How many Jewish people understand what lies before them? How desperately are we seeking to warn people outside the Body of Messiah who have not read the Word of God of what is coming? When Yeshua returns, He will judge us not only by what we have done, but also on the basis of what we have failed to do with what we know.

> **"For the son of Man will come in the glory of His Father with His angels and then He will reward each according to his works."**
> (Matthew 16:27)

Everything we do or fail to do is being recorded even right now in a set of books kept up in heaven.

Why is the area of the right hand and forehead so significant that the anti-Messiah chooses this as the designated site for his mark ? It is here that God commanded we imprint His Word,

> **"You shall bind them as a sign on your hand, and they shall be as a frontlet between your eyes."**
> (Deuteronomy 6:8)

Many Jewish people take this commandment literally and perform a ritual called 'laying teffilin', in which they tie these verses from scripture, hand scribed in Hebrew on parchment and sealed in a small box, upon their forehead with leather straps and bind the straps also around their right arm. Will the Jewish people who practice this ritual refuse to receive the mark of the beast upon these places of their body that are designated as kadosh (set apart and holy) for the Word of God? I suspect that many who are unfortunately unaware of end time prophecies in the New Testament will be caught up with the rest of the world; deceived and drawn towards death through ignorance, pride and rebellion. We see so many these days having their bodies tattooed, even though the Bible prohibits this custom that the goyim (heathens or pagans) practice. If one is already accustomed to taking evil marks on one's body, such as is commonplace today, even amongst Christians, then it seems only a small jump to taking the mark of the beast.

The Help of Man is Useless

This hail storm also opened my eyes to other new revelations. Even in the limited crisis of this storm and tornado, it became painfully obvious that our emergency response system would be woefully inadequate in the event of a more serious emergency. The police force would soon become overwhelmed and it may turn into every man for himself with looting and anarchy, especially in the cities. Those seeking to flee may be trapped and not able to escape. Access routes will be cut off. Families must stick together or they may be separated in this time of trouble and unable to reach each other with help.

We may go through a water crisis if biological warfare is used to infect our water supply. We don't realize how much water we use and how dependent we are on water coming out of our taps until its supply is suddenly cut off. This happened to us in the Negev when a certain pipe malfunctioned. All of a sudden (pit'om in Hebrew), without the slightest warning or preparation time, water stopped flowing out of our taps in the middle of the heat of the Middle Eastern desert. Not only did we lack drinking water; we soon found out that toilets don't flush without water and neither do dirty dishes get washed – not to mention baby's soiled laundry. You can imagine that things didn't smell too good after a while! Residents flocked to the swimming pools to cool off and take a shower. Eventually, a water truck brought drinking water into the middle of the moshav (settlement) so that people could fill up their buckets, but it was obvious that we were woefully unprepared. Even if we store food and water, this supply will only last us so long. Eventually we will run out of food and water. The store shelves will likely be stripped within a very short time. If the big trucks stop supplying the large grocery stores, their shelves will lie empty within two days.

This was one of the Israelites' biggest fear in the desert – where would they find food and water?

> "And the people complained against Moses, saying, "What shall we drink?"
>
> (Exodus 15:24)

They feared that they and their children and livestock would die in the wilderness.

> "And the people thirsted there for water, and the people complained against Moses and said, "Why is it you have brought us up out of Egypt, to kill us and our children and our livestock with thirst?"
>
> (Exodus 18:3)

Again, God provided water, but still the people lived in fear. When it came time to enter the Promised Land and the majority report from the spies was discouraging, the people cried and complained, deciding that heading back to the slavery of Egypt would be a better alternative than being slaughtered by the giants living in the Land.

> "Let us select a leader and return to Egypt!"
>
> (Numbers 14:4)

They had no faith in themselves, in their leader, or in God. Even after seeing all the miracles that God performed through the hand of Moses and Aaron, in their slavery mentality they still distrusted God's goodness, protection, and provision. It was their unbelief that so grieved the heart of God and drove Him to such anger that He vowed to destroy them all, had not Moses stood in the gap for his people, Israel, pleading for divine mercy. The most crucial test of the Israelites, therefore, was not in the matters of physical survival – food and water – these were provided. It was their faith that was tested and found wanting. Even after all the miracles they had witnessed, they still did not trust God. Their hearts were hard through unbelief and rebellion.

> "...they tempted the Lord, saying, "Is the Lord among us or not?"
>
> (Exodus 17:7)

This became the crucial question. This, too, stood as our most formidable enemy in Israel. It was not the giants of the Land, but our own fears, doubts, and lack of faith. As difficulties and challenges continually bombarded us, that niggling thought began to permeate our belief system. Is God really with us in making aliyah?[1] One terrorist attack after another devastated the Israeli people. The whole country lived in a continual state of grief. As the Palestinians danced with glee and gave out candies at the death of our innocents and over the blood of our children running in the streets of Israel, we could not help but wonder, Is God still with Israel? When the Israeli government gave us their decision that we must leave the country within fourteen days, we did not even challenge this unjust ruling. We just assumed that God was not with us; that we might as well turn around and head back to Egypt rather than die here in the wilderness.

So too, during the tribulation, will we be tempted to give up, to give in to the discouragement, despair, oppression, depression and negativity all around us. The love of most will grow cold. Confusion will reign as hasatan[2] takes over in the form of the anti-

---

[1] Aliyah -Hebrew 'to go up', 'to immigrate to the Land of Israel.
[2] hasatan is Hebrew for 'the advesary'

Messiah. The curses (Deuternomy 28) may come into effect in even greater force than presently. As Believers in Yeshua, who redeemed us from the curse of the Torah, having become a curse for us when He hung on the tree (Galatians 3:13), we thought that we'd be immune to the effects of the curses over the Land of Israel due to the people's sin and disobedience to God (according to the terms of the Mosaic Covenant). But we who have entered into the New Covenant found out the hard way, as did other Believers in Israel, that we would also suffer and experience the effects of the curses – sickness, lack, madness, chaos, and even defeat at the hands of our enemies. These curses are a consequence of national sin, and as a result of our identification with the nation of Israel, we also suffered alongside our 'brethren according to the flesh." We must not be naive. Many Christians who stood with the Jewish people during the Holocaust also suffered. The ten Boom family is one example. Corrie ten Boom's father and sister died in the death camps. Her father said it was his privilege to identify with the sufferings of the Jewish people and he also wore the badge of shame – the yellow star of David. When these trials come upon us in the future, we must not then wonder if God is still with us, or not, but rather rejoice that we may share in the sufferings of the Messiah.

> **"Beloved, do not think it strange concerned the fiery trials which is to try you, as though some strange thing happened to you; but rejoice to the extent that you partake of Messiah's sufferings, that when His glory is revealed, you may also be glad with exceeding joy."**
>
> (1 Peter 4:12-13)

If we suffer for righteousness' sake, we are blessed of God. We will need to remember that it is always **"...better, if it is the will of God, to suffer for doing good than for doing evil."** (1 Peter 13:14, 17)

May Your Names be Inscribed in the Book of Life

The word of God says that the Holy Ones will be temporarily given into the enemy's hands under the reign of global terror. (Daniel 7:25) But this is not the end. We must know that we have read the book and are aware of the ending. Yes, there will be a time of trouble come upon the earth. But what happens here on earth is temporal; what really counts is our eternal destiny.

> **"And there shall be a time of trouble, such as never was since there was a nation, even to that time. And at that time your people shall be delivered, every one who is found written in the book."**
>
> (Daniel 12:1-2)

As Jewish people celebrate the Fall Feasts, many send out cards and greetings that their names might be written in the book of life. But how do we move beyond hope to assurance? Yeshua told His disciples that they should not rejoice that demons are subject to them, but rather that their names are written in the book in heaven. (Luke 10:20) Only through the sacrifice of the Messiah, Yeshua, can we know that our sins are forgiven, atonement has been made, therefore we have an everlasting covenant of peace with God (Isaiah 54:10). It is through this New Covenant (Jeremiah 31:31), sealed in the blood of Yeshua (Luke 22:20), that we may know our names are truly inscribed in the Book of Life. What happens to those whose names are not written in the book?

> **"If anyone's name was not found written in the Book of Life, he was thrown into the lake of fire."**
>
> (Revelation 20:15)

Obviously this is a most crucial issue. It is not enough to just 'hope' that our names are written in the book by being 'good enough'. After all, how good is good enough? And if being good gets our names into the Book of Life and a place in Heaven, then why did Yeshua say to the thief on the cross, dying next to him, **"This day you will be with me in Gan Eden** (the Garden of Eden or Paradise)" (Luke 23:43)? Yeshua is the only way back into the Garden of Eden, from which we were expelled for the disobedience of Adam and Eve (Chava). Yeshua restores us to our place in heaven with God. He said,

> **"I am the bread of life (lechem chayim). Your fathers ate the manna in the wilderness, and are dead. This is the bread which comes down from heaven, that one may eat of it and not die. I am the living bread which came down from heaven. If anyone eats of this bread, he will live forever; and the bread that I shall give is My flesh, which I shall give for the life of the world."**
>
> (John 6:48-51)

Leprosy in the Camp

Another error of the Israelites in the wilderness is that they did not respect the anointing on the leadership God had chosen for the camp. Aaron and Miriam spoke against Moses' wife and God struck Miriam with leprosy. We must have a holy fear of speaking against God's anointed ones who take up the position of leadership during the tribulation. The Israelites doubted God's provision and protection. They complained about the food and feared their enemies. They wanted to appoint their own leader and head back. There was division and backbiting in the camp. Korach initiated a rebellion against Moses. He and his followers were swallowed alive by the earth. Are not some of those in Churches and Messianic Congregations biting and devouring one another until they are destroyed?

> "For all the Torah is fulfilled in one word, even in this: You shall love your neighbor as yourself. But if you bite and devour one another, beware lest you be consumed by one another!"
>
> (Galatians 5:14-15)

The leprosy must be cleared out of the camp. Will we continue to debate and argue over doctrinal issues while so many do not have their names written in the Book? We must resolve our spiritual issues of bitterness, rebellion, pride, moral failure, hypocrisy and occult involvement in order to rise up in unity as the people of God He desires for us to be.

Are we going to make the same mistakes as the Israelites did in the wilderness and perish or will we learn from their example and trust God? He is our refuge and strength, our help in time of trouble.

> "God is my refuge and strength;
> A very present help in trouble,
> Therefore we will not fear,
> Even though the earth be removed,
> And though the mountains be carried into the midst of the sea;"
>
> (Psalm 46:1-2)

Will we give in to fear or will we trust God to be our help, our refuge and our strength in the coming time of crisis? While we waited out the storm, Vicki told me about their experience in being stranded in the airport during the blackout on the east coast. She testified to the grace and favor of God in providing for them during this time of trouble. Although many were weeping and sleeping on the bare floor (all the hotel rooms in the area were understandably booked), Vicki felt led to call a certain hotel which was brand new. "Do you have any rooms?", she asked. "Yes, what kind of room would you like?" was the surprising reply. Many people had been stranded with no money or food. All electricity had been cut off so the electric stoves and ovens would not operate in the restaurants. She walked down the street and someone beckoned her to come in to a Pizzeria. "We have a gas stove," they said. "Come in and we'll feed you pizza."

Supernatural Protection

God's word promises supernatural protection and provision to those who are in covenant relationship with Him. I spoke to John, an elderly friend of mine who owns a farm nearby. He called to see how we fared during the storm. Amazingly, not one piece of hail fell on his property. They only received a brief and mild rain during the night. The scripture immediately popped into my mind from the account of the ten plagues upon Egypt.

> **"And the hail struck throughout the whole land of Egypt, all that was in the field...Only in the land of Goshen, where the children of Israel were, there was no hail."**
>
> (Exodus 9:25-26)

The land of Goshen was set apart by God because His covenant people dwelt there. Also when the plague of flies hit Egypt, there were no flies in Goshen. Why? Because God makes a distinction between His people and Egypt. (Exodus 8:22-23) This does not mean that God shows favoritism; it means He honors covenant. It is not only Jewish people who may come under God's shelter of protection and provision. Peter said,

> "God shows no partiality. But in every nation whoever fears Him and works righteousness is accepted by Him."
>
> (Acts 10:34-35)

The book of Ephesians tells us that Gentiles who were once far away from God, without God and without hope in the world, outside the place of covenant, excluded from the blessings and protection this covenant gives, have been brought near to God through the blood of the Jewish Messiah, Yeshua (Jesus). (Ephesians 2:19) They have taken refuge under the shelter of His wings, as did the Moabitess, Ruth. Boaz prayed that she would be given a full reward by the Lord God of Israel, **"under whose wings you have taken refuge."**(Ruth 2:12) Have you as yet taken refuge under the wings of the Almighty, the Lord God of Israel? There is no time to lose! The storm is on its way. Even in Egypt, those who feared the word of the Lord brought their cattle indoors and were spared. But those who did not, suffered the full judgment of the plague of hail.[3]

> **"He who feared the word of the Lord among the servants of Pharaoh made his servants and his livestock flee to the houses. But he who did not regard the word of the Lord left his servants and his livestock in the field."**
>
> (Exodus 9:20-21)

And the hail destroyed them.

---

3 For a more complete explanation, see book, Messiah Revealed in the Passover.

Running The Race

The day of the storm, our city held a triathlon. Many athletes were caught out in the hail, wind, and rain. Physical fitness is of some benefit for this life, but we need to be even more concerned about whether or not we are fit for the life to come.

> **"For bodily exercise profits a little, but godliness is profitable for all things, having promise of the life that now is and of that which is to come."**
>
> (1Timothy 4:8)

This scripture does not let couch potatoes off the hook, nor people like me who hate to exercise, but the truth is that those who run their races for an earthly prize (a perishable crown) alone will find it no consolation when the wrath of God falls upon the earth. But we are to run the race set before us with endurance, running to win the prize of a heavenly (imperishable) crown. (Hebrews 12:1; 1Corinthians 9:24) Some of the runners scurried in under the shelter to, by necessity, join our congregational picnic. Drenched with rain and hail, they dried off and warmed up by the fire someone had started in the stone hearth. Many who are now outside a covenantal relationship with the God of Israel will come running when the plagues hit during the tribulation. They will seek provision, warmth, and protection from the Body of Messiah. What was most beautiful to experience was the spirit of love and unity that pervaded our group in the shelter. It felt so good to lend a jacket to cover a baby that had no blanket - to sing hymns to those who were fearful, to share everything we had together for the common good. This was the manner of the first believers – love in action. What good are we, James writes, if we see a brother in physical need and don't extend ourselves to him in practical ways? (James 2:14-17) I hope and believe that this spirit will again rise up among Believers to show the love of God to those who seek shelter amongst us and to one another during the coming time of trouble. Without Vicki and Robert's wisdom in being prepared and equipped along with their generosity to share what provisions they had with us, we could have been in much greater distress. I deeply appreciated their parents' doting kindness towards my children. The elderly will also have an important role to contribute to the community of Believers during the tribulation.

The Shofar Call

Perhaps all this talk about the time of tribulation is causing worry, fear or anxiety. If only the thought of what may happen sends us reeling, what will become of us when it actually happens? For this reason, it is crucial, especially at the time of the Fall Feasts, which is traditionally a time to examine our inner selves, confess areas of sin, go to others who may have something against us and make peace with our brothers and sisters. The shofar calls us to wake up and take stock of our spiritual condition, what darkness lies hidden in our hearts, to seek the Lord and turn from any wicked ways He reveals within us.

> **"If we confess our sins, He is faithful and just to forgive us our sins and to cleanse us from all unrighteousness."**
>
> (1 John 1:9)

Alternatively, the ones who cover or hide their sins will not prosper according to the Word of God. Now is the perfect time to deepen our relationship with the Lord, cleanse our hearts and immerse ourselves in the precious Word of God. We must know without doubt in our hearts that our relationship with Him and with others is right – that He is with us; He will protect us, deliver us and provide for us.

> "Why should I fear in the days of evil, when the iniquity at my heels surrounds me?"
>
> (Psalms 49:5)

Why should we fear when the anti-Messiah takes his place in the temple in Jerusalem and declares himself God and the whole world falls into deception to worship him and take the mark of the beast? We need not fear. God is with us.

> "Be still and know that I am God; I will be exalted among the nations, I will be exalted in the earth! The Lord of hosts (יהוה צבאות Adonay T'zvaot) is with us; The God of Jacob (Elohei Yaacov) is our refuge."
>
> (Psalm 46:10-11)

We must hide these words in our heart now, so that they may comfort and re-assure us in the coming time of Jacob's trouble. As I waited in the shelter, watching my baby sleeping peacefully and my girls giggling from under their warm blankets, with the storm raging all about us, I reflected on the goodness of God in providing a shelter for us.

> "For You have been a shelter for me, a strong tower from the enemy.
> I will abide in Your tabernacle forever; I will trust in the shelter of Your wings."
>
> (Psalm 61:3)

To face the tribulation outside the shelter of His wings will be a terrible thing. Disobedience can take us outside this shelter, as can rebellion or any willful sin. Yeshua wept over Jerusalem, knowing its impending destruction. He wanted to be a shelter and refuge for them but they were not willing. He said,

> "O Jerusalem, Jerusalem, the one who kills the prophets and stones those who are sent to her! How often I wanted to gather your children together, as a hen gathers her chicks under her wings, but you were not willing!"
>
> (Matthew 23:37)

There is only one ultimate place of shelter and that is a place in the New Covenant with the Almighty God through His son, Yeshua (Jesus). The blood of the Passover lamb protected the Israelites from the destroyer. It is the same today. We must stay covered, by faith, with the blood of the Lamb of God. Even today, most of Jerusalem is unwilling to come under this shelter and they will face a terrible time of trouble, but the word of God says they will be saved out of it (though with many losses).

> "And it is the time of Jacob's trouble, but he shall be saved out of it."
>
> (Jeremiah 30:7)

God honors covenant. He will save and defend Jerusalem from all the nations that come against her in the end times.

The balance to this issue of preparing for the end times is that to sit and do nothing if the Holy Spirit is prompting action is disobedience. Some may say, "Oh, I don't have to prepare; God will take care of us." Yes, God will definitely need to supernaturally intervene to care for us during the tribulation, but if the Holy Spirit gives divine guidance on steps we may take beforehand, then we would be foolish to ignore His wisdom.

Wisdom calls aloud and raises her voice, but fools will not listen, to which wisdom replies,

> "Because I have called and you refused, I have stretched out my hand and no one regarded because you disdained all my counsel, and would have none of my rebuke, I also will laugh at your calamity; I will mock when your terror comes, when your terror comes like a storm and your destruction comes like a whirlwind, when distress and anguish come upon you…they would have none of my counsel and despised my every rebuke. Therefore they shall eat the fruit of their own way…for the turning away of the simple will slay them and the complacency of fools will destroy them; But whoever listens to me will dwell safely, and will be secure, without fear of evil."
>
> (Proverbs 1:20-33)

Will we allow the strident call of the shofar to shake us out of complacency to hear the voice of the Holy Spirit and follow His wisdom, leading us to safety? Or will it be calamity, terror and destruction that will move us?

If we can foresee the signs indicating an evil time about to come upon us, then prudence should compel us to find a hiding place until these calamities have passed us by – or at least a way of helping others to survive.

> "A prudent man foresees evil and hides himself; the simple pass on and are punished."
>
> (Proverbs 27:12)

When the Spirit of God revealed to Joseph the meaning of Pharaoh's dream – the coming of seven years of plenty followed by seven years of famine – Joseph immediately rallied Egypt to prepare by storing food. What if Joseph had sat back and said, "No worries; God will take care of us." Certainly many lives would not have been saved through his foresight and wisdom, even the lives of his own brothers and father. The lives of our own kin, our sisters and brothers, mother and father, and many others may depend on our obedience to the Holy Spirit. We may need to prepare a place of refuge and provision, not only for ourselves but also for them. Like Lot's sons in law, they may scoff at our warnings and be left to face God's judgment. But at least we would have tried. There are others who may simply be woefully unaware of the end time prophecies. Noah also prepared an ark for the saving of his family when God warned him of the flood that was on its way.

> **"By faith, Noah, being divinely warned of things not yet seen, moved with godly fear, prepared an ark for the saving of his household…"**
> (Hebrews 11:7)

We do not need to be alarmists, but then again, we had better be ready to move in godly fear when God says move!
There are some who will not move because of their reluctance to give up the passing pleasures and temporary comforts of this world. Their homes and possessions will hold them in bondage. But, like Moses, we would do well to choose to suffer affliction with the people of God rather than indulge in the riches and treasures of 'Egypt'. We must keep ourselves focused on the reward. (Hebrews 11:25-26) Those who hold fast to their faith and overcome the tribulation will inherit a heavenly crown; (Rev. 3:11) they will be clothed with white garments and their names will not be blotted out from the Book of Life. (Rev. 3:5) They will receive the name of God, the name of God's city, the New Jerusalem, and a new name for themselves.(Rev. 3:12) They will be granted a place of honor sitting with the Lord on His throne. (Rev. 3:21). What a reward to look forward to! The tribulation will not last forever – only

2520 days. We can count them. Knowing that the tribulation is temporary and keeping our eyes on Yeshua, the author and finisher of our faith, we can endure. As long as we dwell under the shelter of God's covenant we will remain secure.

> **"He who dwells in the secret place of the Most High (Elyon) shall abide under the shadow of the Almighty (Shaddai). I will say of the Lord, "He is my refuge and my fortress; My God, in Him I will trust."…He shall cover you with His feathers, and under His wings you shall take refuge;…You shall not be afraid of the terror by night, nor of the arrow that flies by day…a thousand may fall at your side, and ten thousand at your right hand; but it shall not come near you. Only with your eyes shall you look and see the reward of the wicked. Because you have made the Lord, who is my refuge, even the Most High, your dwelling place, no evil shall befall you, nor shall any plague come near your dwelling; For He shall give His angels charge over you, to keep you in all your ways."**
>
> (Psalm 91:1-11)

Come now under the warm, safe, and dry shelter of the wings of Shaddai, Elyon, through a relationship with Yeshua the Messiah, His son. God promises to keep us safe in His Sukkah (tabernacle or temporary shelter) when the days are evil.

> **"For in the time of trouble**
> **He shall hide me in His Sukkah**
> **In the secret place of His tabernacle**
> **He shall hide me;**
> **He shall set me high upon a rock."**
>
> (Psalm 27:5)

Added Insurance Coverage

There is one final thing that we may do as an added 'insurance policy' in preparing to face the tribulation. What may we do to ensure our position of favor with the Lord and enjoy the privilege of His protection? If we look at the account of the fall of Yericho, we will see that only one family survived the destruction of the city. Was it the most righteous family? The richest? The one with the highest social position? On the contrary, the woman who ensured the survival of her family was a harlot named Rahab. What did she do? She aided Israel. She knew and feared God and helped hide the Israeli spies on her rooftop. For this kindness, Joshua agreed to spare her and her whole family.

> **"And Joshua spared Rahab the harlot, her father's household, and all that she had. So she dwells in Israel to this day, because she hid the messengers whom Joshua sent o spy out Yericho."**
>
> (Joshua 6:25)

We can also notice, in another example, that a Gentile, Moabite woman named Ruth gained the favor of the Kinsman Redeemer, Boaz. She asked,

> **"Why have I found favor in your eyes, that you should take notice of me, since I am a foreigner."**
>
> (Ruth 2:10)

What was his answer? It was because it had been "fully reported to him" the kindness she showed to her mother-in-law, Naomi. Ruth had pledged,

> **"Your people will be my people and your God my God."**
>
> (Ruth 1:16)

Boaz is a type of the Messiah as our Redeemer. Noami represents those Jewish survivors who have returned to the Land of Israel after losing their families and all their possessions in the Holocaust. Ruth represents the Gentile Church, joined by covenant with Israel through the Messiah. We may rest assured that any acts of kindness shown to the people of Israel is fully reported to our Redeemer and gains His notice and favor.[4]

We know that all the nations will one day, perhaps soon, come against Israel and Jerusalem. At the point of this writing, the government of Israel has disobeyed God's warning not to make a treaty with the people of the Land. They continue to give up more and more territories that God has given, by everlasting covenant, to the people of Israel. This can only mean trouble. Today, another devastating terrorist attack hit Israel in Be'er Sheva. Suicide bombers blew up two buses at once, killing many Israelis and injuring scores of others. As a desperate attempt to protect its citizens, Israel is now building a wall to separate itself from the Palestinians. The world charges Israel with apartheid and racism. The nations, under the deception of the devil, will not be satisfied until Israel is completely annihilated. Perhaps once the wall is completed and the territories given to the Arabs against the stated will of God, they will think they are safe. But they have used the ways of man, trusting in the shelter of Egypt (Isaiah 30) rather than trust in the protective shelter of obedience to God's Word. When they say, Peace and safety, then destruction will come suddenly!

> **"For when they say, "Peace and safety!" then sudden destruction comes upon them, as labor pains upon a pregnant woman. And they shall not escape."**
>
> (1Thessalonians 5:3)

---

[4] See the emotionally stirring video, Ruth a Righteous Gentile for Hannah's complete message on this subject.

We must remember that Yeshua came for the lost sheep of the House of Israel and still considers them His Brethren. He will separate the sheep and the goats, determining their eternal destiny depending on how we care for even the least of His brethren. (Mathew 25:39-end) And yet what proportion of the Christian Church today is apathetic or even unaware of their relationship to Israel or their spiritual debt of gratitude towards the Jewish people for the Messiah and the Word of God. How many will turn in the Jews who seek a hiding place, rather than give them refuge? How many have pledged, Your God is my God, but fail to acknowledge their relationship with His people? Because Gentile Christians have received so great a spiritual treasure, they have an obligation, the apostle Paul states, to give materially, especially to the Jewish Believers (the poor Saints in Jerusalem - Romans 15:27). If we seek added "insurance coverage", we would do well to show kindness to Israel, to give generously in material ways, and to remain faithful to the nation of Israel and the Jewish people, even if the whole world turns against her, even if it costs us our lives.

Golden Kackie

The gold that the Israelites in the desert plundered from Egypt and made into a golden idolatrous calf ended up a human waste product (I'm being polite here). Moses ground the golden calf into a powder and made the Israelites drink it. In Israel, we call human waste product kackie. All their gold turned to kackie when it became their idol. If riches come, may we never set out sights on them, but keep our focus on the Lord and His Kingdom.

This is not a day to trust in riches, for riches cannot deliver from death, but only righteousness through the Messiah Yeshua. (Proverbs 11:4) Riches will do us no good in the coming tribulation; it will not be able to buy our protection against the wrath of God.

(Psalm 49: 6-7) If we can neither buy nor sell, then possessing all the gold and silver in the world will do us no good. No one can 'buy' protection against God's wrath.

> **"Neither their silver nor their gold shall be able to deliver them in the day of the Lord's wrath; but the whole land shall be devoured by the fire of His jealousy, for He will make speedy riddance of all those who dwell in the land."**
>
> (Zephaniah 1:18)

Only the blood of Yeshua is powerful enough to save us from the wrath of God. It makes no sense to ponder what commodity will be best to invest in to secure our future. God and silver will profit us nothing.

> **"Come now, you rich, weep and howl for your miseries that are coming upon you! Your riches are corrupted, and your garments are moth-eaten. Your gold and silver are corroded, and their corrosion will be a witness against you and will eat your flesh like fire. You have heaped up treasure in the last days."**
>
> (James 5:1-3)

Those who live in pleasure and luxury, giving no thought to laying up, instead, their treasure in heaven by giving to the poor and to the work of the Lord in these last days will find that they placed their trust in a useless idol. This is the time for those who have been blessed with riches in this day to give generously to the Kingdom of God and to be rich in good deeds.

> "Command those who are rich in this present age not to be haughty, nor to trust in uncertain riches but in the living God, who gives us richly all things to enjoy. Let them do good, that they be rich in good works, ready to give, willing to share, storing up for themselves a good foundation for the time to come, that they may lay hold on eternal life."
>
> (1 Timothy 6:17)

Now is not the time to be gathering up treasure for ourselves here on earth, but instead laying up treasure in heaven. (Matthew 19:21) It is not the time to labor only for food to fill our bellies but to labor for the harvest, for the Kingdom of God.

> "Do not labor for the food which perishes, but for the food which endures to everlasting life, which the Son of Man will give you, because God the Father has set His seal on Him."
>
> (John 6: 27)

In The End

In the end, we may be forced to take to living again like the Israelites in the wilderness, dwelling in tents and trusting in God for our very survival. Each time we celebrate Sukkot is to be a dress rehearsal for this time. It was never meant to be a token sukkah (booth) set up on a balcony or in one's yard to sit in for a couple hours of schmoozing and nashing (visiting and eating). We are to live in temporary shelters for seven days and remember our days of wandering in the desert and the lessons we were supposed to have learned. Ephraim boasts of his wealth, "Surely I have become rich, I have found wealth for myself, in all my labors they shall find in me no iniquity that is sin." But God answers with the statement that He is Elohim.

> **"I am the Lord your God, ever since the land of Egypt; I will again make you dwell in tents as in the days of the appointed feast (mo'ed)."**
> (Hosea 12:8-9)

Despite all the trials and tribulations we will endure on this earth and perhaps in our lifetime, our comfort is found in the last book of the Bible, the book of Revelation. Finally will come the joyous fulfillment of Sukkot (Tabernacles) - when this earth has passed away and the New Jerusalem comes down out of heaven from God, prepared as a bride adorned for her husband. The prophet describing his vision hears a loud voice from heaven saying,

> **"Behold the tabernacle of God is with men, and He will dwell with them, and they shall be His people. God Himself will be with them and be their God. And God will wipe away every tear from their eyes; there shall be no more death, nor sorrow, nor crying. There shall be no more pain, for the former things have passed away."**
> (Revelation 21:1-4)

> **"The Lamb is the light of this magnificent city and there will be no more curse. Nothing and no one will enter it who will defile or cause an abomination or a lie, but only those who are written in the Lamb's Book of Life."**
> (Revelation 21:23, 27, 22:3)

Shalom and may your name be inscribed in the Lamb's Book of Life for eternity!

CHAPTER FIVE

GOD'S APPOINTED TIMES FOR JEW AND GENTILE

Where will the Church stand with regards to Israel in the end times? It is only out of ignorance that so many remain disinterested or even hostile towards Israel. A growing segment of the Church is accepting world opinion and bowing to a humanistic view of the situation in the Middle East in pitying and siding with the 'plight of the Palestinians'. Although God has His faithful remnant that oppose this trend, a portion of the Church, even the very elect, are being deceived into standing against God in His purposes towards Israel. The non-Jewish Church must come to understand and accept their relationship towards the nation of Israel.

Citizenship in the Commonwealth of Israel

The Word says that those who were once called 'Not My people' will also join in the privilege of being called God's people.

> **"I will show My love to the one I called 'Not My loved one'. I will say to those called 'Not My people', 'You are My people' and they will say, 'You are my God.'"**
>
> (Hosea 2:23)

How was this feat accomplished? Those who were once far away have been brought near through the blood of the Jewish Messiah.

> "Remember that at that time you were separate from the Messiah, excluded from citizenship in Israel and foreigners to the covenants of the promise, without hope and without God in the world. But now in the Messiah Yeshua you who once were far away have been brought near through the blood of Messiah... Consequently, you are no longer foreigners and aliens, but fellow citizens with God's people and members of God's household."
>
> (Ephesians 2:11-19)

Do the 'gerim' - the ones who were once strangers - realise the privilege of now being able to count themselves included as fellow citizens with Israel and part of the covenant that the Jewish people have enjoyed with God for centuries? Can we accept that the transgression of Israel has led to the salvation of the Gentiles? (Rom. 11:11) Do we understand that the wild olive shoots have been grafted in among the others and now share in the nourishing sap from the olive root? (Rom. 11:17) Paul warned Gentile believers not to boast over the natural branches (Rom 11:18) and not to be ignorant of the mystery so that they may not be conceited.

> "Israel has experienced a hardening in part until the full number of the Gentiles has come in. And so all Israel will be saved."
>
> (Romans 11:25-26)

The new covenant was originally given to the house of Israel and the house of Judah.

> "'The time is coming,' declares the Lord, 'when I will make a new covenant with the house of Israel and with the house of Judah.'"
>
> (Jeremiah 31:31)

Yeshua states that He was sent only to the lost sheep of Israel (Matt. 15:24). But the ancient prophets knew that the Messiah would also be a light to the Gentiles and would bring His salvation (yeshuah) to the whole world.

> "It is too small a thing for You to be My Servant to restore the tribes of Jacob and bring back those of Israel I have kept. I will also make You a light for the Gentiles, that You may bring My salvation to the ends of the earth."
>
> (Isaiah 49:6)

Temporary Blindness in God's Plan

It was within God's plan for this temporary blindness to be over the eyes of the Jewish people in order that the full number of the Gentiles could come into the Kingdom of God. Should the Church not be walking in humility and gratitude towards the Jewish people instead of in ignorance and arrogance, calling them 'Christ Killers' and other choice names? Rivers of Jewish blood have flowed thanks to those who called themselves Christians, but who tortured, raped and murdered the first covenant people of God. The Crusades, the Spanish Inquisition, the Russian pogroms, and the European Holocaust were all carried out 'in the name of Christ'.[1]

---

[1] See Richard Booker's book, "When the Cross Became a Sword", or Michael Brown's book, "Our Hands are Stained with Blood." Destiny Image Publisher.

The Final Judgement

In chapter 25 of the book of Matthew, Yeshua tells about the Final Judgment.

> "When the Son of Man comes in His glory, and all the angels with Him, He will sit on His throne in heavenly glory. All the nations will be gathered before Him, and He will separate the people one from another as a shepherd separates the sheep from the goats. He will put the sheep on His right and the goats on His left."
>
> (Matthew 25:31-33)

The sheep on His right (called the righteous) will be invited to take their inheritance – eternal life in the kingdom of God. The goats on His left, which are cursed, will be banished into the eternal fire prepared for the devil and his angels. Just how does the Lord judge between the sheep and the goats? To the righteous, He says,

> "For I was hungry and you gave Me something to eat, I was thirsty and you gave Me something to drink, I was a stranger and you invited Me in, I needed clothes and you clothed Me, I was sick and you looked after Me, I was in prison and you came to visit Me."
>
> (Matthew 25:35-36)

Then the righteous will answer the Lord that they don't recall ever seeing Him hungry or thirsty, needing clothes or shelter, sick or imprisoned.

> **"The King will reply, "I tell you the truth, whatever you did for one of the least of these brothers of Mine, you did for Me."**
>
> (Matthew 25:40)

Who are the King's brothers? At the time He walked the face of this earth as Yeshua, His brothers were the Jews. When a Canaanite woman came to Him crying for mercy for her demon-possessed daughter, the Lord answered,

> **"I was sent only to the lost sheep of Israel."**
>
> (Matthew 15:24)

Yad Vashem, the Holocaust Memorial Museum in Jerusalem boasts rows and rows of trees growing in the 'Avenue of the Righteous Gentiles'. One tree has been planted for each Gentile person who provided food, drink, shelter, clothing, medical care and compassion to those Jewish victims of the Holocaust. Many lost their lives for giving even a crust of bread to a Jew. Thank you. Thank you. You are blessed by the Father; the kingdom has been prepared for you since the creation of the world. Thank God for people like Corrie Ten Boom and her family, who considered it a privilege to suffer in a concentration camp and even die for the sake of helping even one Jewish child.

But woe to those who closed their ears to the cries of the Jews entrapped like animals in cattle cars on their way to the gas chambers. Too often, those standing beside the trains ignored or even mocked and laughed at the Jews' tortured pleas for a simple drink of water. To them, the Lord will say,

> **"Whatever you did not do for one of the least of these, you did not do for Me."**
>
> (Matthew 25:45)

We cannot change the past, but we can learn from it. I believe that the Lord is going to give His people one last redemptive opportunity to prove themselves righteous. Just as Herzl warned the Jews of Europe to get out and flee to Palestine before it was too late, many modern-day prophets in several nations are now warning the Jews of the Diaspora, especially the North Americans, to hurry home. Most of them, as before, will not listen. They are too comfortable, too occupied with this earthly material life to be concerned with spiritual matters.

A prophecy is being issued that a terrible disaster will shortly fall upon the Jews outside the land of Israel. Whether this is another wave of persecution under the rule of the anti-Christ or something else, I'm not sure. But the Lord has promised that He *will* bring the Jewish people back to the land of Israel from the North, the South, the East, *and* the *West*. Just as it took the hand of God's wrath to deliver the Israelites out of the land of Egypt, so does God promise that He will bring them out of every land with outpoured wrath.

> **"I will bring you from the nations and gather you from the countries where you have been scattered – with a mighty hand and an outstretched arm and with outpoured wrath."**
>
> (Ezekiel 20:34)

Christians around the world are being prepared by the Holy Spirit to help these Jews as they flee from the nations of exile and struggle to return to the land of Israel. May you also be blessed with the opportunity to give food, drink, shelter, medical aid, and compassion to these brothers of our Lord. Seek God for what part He may have you play in His wonderful plan of the redemption and salvation of His people, Israel.[2]

---

2 See Tom Hess's book, "Let My People Go!" Progresive Vision Publishers.

CHAPTER SIX

THE RELATIONSHIP OF CHRISTIANS TO ISRAEL

A Call to Repentance

I believe that the people of God also need to examine their relationship and attitude towards Israel and the Jewish people. There exists a terrible apathy and ignorance, if not outright hostility in the mainstream Christian Church in this area. Many believe that they have replaced Israel in God's sight and affection, and therefore Israel is no longer of consequence to them. Others just place Israel into one more slot among all the nations in their 'missionary program'. I am generalizing, of course, and there are many individual Christians who love and support Israel and the Jewish people and some churches are even holding prayer for Israel meetings. I hope that those who do not fit into this apathetic and anti-Semitic segment will not feel judged and will forgive me.

The Jerusalem Post carried an article about the torching of three American synagogues.[1] Who was responsible for the carrying out of this anti-Semitic destruction? Serbian 'so-called' Christians who blame the Jews for the bombing of their country and for

---

[1] June 20th, 1999

'taking over the world'! The message about God's everlasting love for Israel and Christians' responsibility to the Jewish people, as outlined in scripture desperately needs to reach people such as these.

A Day of Vengeance – For Zion's Sake

The Word, however, gives another reason for God's judgement being poured out upon the nations – in vengeance for Zion. Almost every nation, including Canada and the U.S., holds a shameful record of how they treated the Jewish people as they wandered in the lands of their exile and especially just before, during, and after the period of the Holocaust. As the nations have treated the Jews, so will the Lord treat the nations.

> **"The day of the Lord is near for all nations. As you have done, it will be done to you; your deeds will return upon your own head."**
>
> (Obadiah 1:15)

Not only have the nations mistreated the Jews in the past; the Word of God prophecies that all nations will come against Jerusalem in the future. The Lord, Himself will fight against these nations, and will strike them with a plague.

> **"For I will gather all the nations to battle against Jerusalem... Then the Lord will go forth and fight against those nations, as He fights in the day of battle... And this shall be the plague with which the Lord will strike all the people who fought against Jerusalem..."**
>
> (Zech. 14:2, 3, 12)

The Lord has an urgent message for the people of the nations of the earth. Are they listening?

> **"Come near, you nations, and listen; pay attention, you peoples... The Lord is angry with all nations; His wrath is upon all their armies. He will totally destroy them... For the Lord has a day of vengeance, a year of retribution, *to uphold Zion's cause.*"**
>
> (Isaiah 34:1-8)

The only hope of the nations is fervent and sincere repentance. Christians, as a kingdom of priests, must lead the way. This year, in the past two months alone Christian leaders organized three international conferences on the theme of Christian repentance towards the Jews. Hundreds of Christians, led by a nun who grew up in Nazi Germany, came to Jerusalem to publicly confess the role that Christian anti-Semitism played in the Holocaust. Sister Pista, of the protestant interdenominational Evangelical Sisterhood of Mary, gave this quote in the Jerusalem Post, *"Six million Jews perished because of thousands of bible-believing Christian like me who had been deceived and went along with the flow."*[2]

Now is definitely not the time to 'go with the flow' of the world system and its ungodly views. Christians around the world are hearing in the Spirit the shofar alarm call of God to repent.

---

2 View video, "Voice Out of Zion II (Where is Your Brother Jacob?)", for an interview with a sister from the conference.

Intercessors – Watchmen on the Walls

God's eternal dominion of the earth will centre in and emanate from Jerusalem, the capital of this nation. God's Word promises this land to the Jewish people. Christians need to stand with tiny Israel with much intercessory and financial support as they defend their right to the land against all the Muslim, Arab nations surrounding them. I am, frankly, tired of hearing all the support for a Palestinian state within Israel coming from Christian sources. The people who have 'the book' should know better than this. If they fail the test, they will be able to offer no excuse, for it has always been an open book exam. God has posted watchmen on the walls of Jerusalem. The Hebrew word for Christians is notzrim. This word also means 'watchmen'.

> **"I have posted watchmen on your walls, O Jerusalem; they will never be silent day or night. You who call on the Lord, give yourselves no rest, and give Him no rest till He establishes Jerusalem and makes her the praise of the earth."**
>
> (Isaiah 62:6-7)

Are the watchmen and women at their posts, calling upon the Lord for Zion's sake, or are they resting?

Sharing Material Blessings

Not only are Gentile Christians to be interceding on behalf of Israel and the Jewish people, they are also, according to the exhortation of Paul, to be giving financially to support Israel and the Jews.

> **"For if the Gentiles have shared in the Jews' spiritual blessings, they owe it to the Jews to share with them their material blessings."**
>
> (Romans 15:27)

Yes, the scriptures are actually talking about money here. The Gentiles, through the blood of the Jewish Messiah, now share spiritual blessings – salvation, hope, a place in the covenant family of God, a Saviour, and the bible. In order to repay this tremendous debt, Gentiles are exhorted to share their finances with the Jews. Those who do not are not only in ignorance or rebellion, but they are also denying themselves a blessing. God's promise to Abraham and his descendants still holds true today:

> **"I will bless those who bless you, and whoever curses you I will curse."**
>
> (Genesis 12:3)

If you want to experience a greater blessing from the Lord, start blessing Israel and the Jewish people today, but especially the Messianic Jewish remnant in the Land. We recently experienced this Christian love in action in Ariel, capital of Samaria, where we lived at one time in Israel. A group from Denver Colorado brought a team of singers to sing to the Jewish, Israeli crowd songs of hope in the God of Israel. The evening was also a tribute to the handicapped soldiers – those who sacrificed their once strong, healthy, bodies to defend this tiny nation of Israel against all its enemies. In their wheelchairs, they danced on stage and we all wept. A delegation of soldiers cheered them on.

The Internationals – two beautiful, Christian men and women – sang almost the complete program in Hebrew (with no accent, yet!). I can only imagine the time and effort it took these devoted servants of the Lord to learn all these familiar songs in Hebrew – to convey their love and dedication to the people of Israel, as well as their God. The crowd loved them. They encouraged this mass of weary, frustrated people, *"Do not be discouraged. Do not give up. We love you"*, and they sang, 'Keep the Candle burning' and 'Miracles' from the movie Prince of Egypt. They did not preach Jesus; rather, they told the people that our God is a God of miracles and we must keep believing. Truly these people fulfilled the exhortation to:

> **"Strengthen the feeble hands, steady the knees that give way; say to those with fearful hearts, 'Be strong, do not fear; your God will come, He will come with vengeance; with divine retribution He will come to save you.'"**
>
> (Isaiah 35:3-4)

The leader of this team then handed a cheque to the delegate from the government of Ariel for $30,000 to help new olim (immigrants) integrate into Israeli society and educational system. Faith Bible Chapel also maintains an afternoon centre for disabled children next to my son's kindergarten. What wonderful, glorious obedience to the revelation of scripture these people have received about repaying the debt they owe the Jews. I know the Holy Spirit was well pleased and many hearts were touched during this evening performance. Through demonstrating the love of God to His people like this are helping to break down that dividing wall that has been built up between Jews and Gentiles.

Priority to the Saints

Unfortunately, very little, if any of these funds came into the hands of the Messianic Jews. At the same time that this group of Christians handed such a sum over to the city leaders, we were down at the city's offices, desperately trying to obtain even a couple of hundred shekels (about $50 U.S.) to purchase a used washing machine. We had made aliyah to Israel and came with only our two suitcases each and the clothes on our backs. And so I urge you to read the context of the apostle Paul's exhortation to Gentiles to share their material resources with the Jews. He specifies to the 'saints' in Jerusalem – the Believers.

> **"Now, however, I am on my way to Jerusalem in the service of the saints there. For Macedonia and Achaia were pleased to make a contribution for the poor <u>among the saints</u> in Jerusalem."**
>
> (Romans 15:25-26)

This should always take priority over giving to the secular government or the non-believing segment of Israeli society. As much as it may gratify us to give to the non-believer, our first priority must be to see the spread of the good news about Yeshua to the Jewish people. In supporting the Messianic Jewish remnant in the land, there exists a greater chance of reaching our own people with the Messiah in a Jewish cultural context that our people can more easily recognise and identify with. In giving to Orthodox Jewish causes, organizations, ministries, and yeshivas (rabbinical training centres), sincere Christians may not realize that they could be supporting the very ones that persecute their brothers and sisters in the Lord.

Spies for Yeshua

We once 'spied in on' a seminar designed to teach the Jews how to 'protect' themselves from Christian or Messianic 'missionaries'. It showed Messianic Jews in a terribly distorted light and presented a truly evil picture of our intents and purposes. In the back of the synagogue that they were teaching in was a huge bookcase with a gold plaque over the top, which read, "This bookcase was donated by Christian friends of............." How much more eternal fruit could these funds have produced had they been given to the Messianic body in Israel rather than for a set of bookshelves for an Orthodox Jewish synagogue that sponsored an anti-Yeshua seminar? In wanting to demonstrate love towards the Jews, one must not neglect the priority towards one's own family. This is like a pastor giving all his time and energy to his ministry for God, but neglecting his wife and children in the process. I don't believe that this brings glory to God.

The Unbroken Covenant

At this time of the Fall Feasts, we need to examine our hearts and lives and repent of any traces of anti-Semitic attitudes or actions. Many people, even those in Christian leadership, justify their anti-Semitic attitudes towards the Jewish people by believing that since they 'rejected Christ', God is finished with the Jews. The Word of God, however, speaks of God's faithfulness towards His first covenant people.

> **"This is what the Lord says; 'Only if the heavens above can be measured and the foundations of the earth below be searched out will I reject all the descendants of Israel because of all they have done."**
> (Jeremiah 31:37)

Yes, Israel has sinned; for this they have been punished severely. But God's love towards His people is not based upon their faithfulness, but upon His own.

> **"For the sake of His great name the Lord will not reject His people, because the Lord was pleased to make you His own."**
> (1 Samuel 12:22)

If God can so easily break covenant with His people based on their behavior, how can we, as new covenant believers, remain assured that God would not break covenant with us? God is not a covenant breaker – He is a faithful, covenant-keeping God.

> **"I will not violate My covenant or alter what My lips have uttered."**
>
> (Psalm 89:34)

If God has not rejected the Jewish people, then neither should the people who follow the Jewish Messiah! Only the Holy Spirit can remove hatred and replace it with love. Satan wants to destroy the Jewish people; God wants to save them. Choose to be on God's side and remain faithful to your Jewish brothers and sisters, even in their present hardness to the good news of salvation through Yeshua.

Spiritual Adultery

Unfortunately, due to anti-Semitism in the Christian Church, and following after the traditions of men, rather than the ways of God, most Christians have disassociated themselves from their Jewish roots, and have even attached themselves to the unholy root which is Babylon.

Yeshua prophesies that

> **"True worshipers will worship the Father in spirit and truth, for they are the kind of worshipers the Father seeks. God is Spirit, and His worshipers must worship in spirit and in truth."**
>
> (John 4:23-24)

True worshipers will worship the *Father*, not the Spirit or the Son. Today in most churches, we hear prayer, praise and worship directed towards Jesus, but Yeshua never accepted personal worship or glory;

> "'Why do you call Me good?' Yeshua answered. 'No one is good – except God alone.'"
>
> (Mark 10:18)

He always directed the people's worship to the Father:

> "I am the way and the truth and the life. No one comes to the Father except <u>through Me</u>."
>
> (John 14:6)

We come *through*, Yeshua *to* the Father. We are not to be creating images and statues of Yeshua, Mary, or anyone else to worship, but are to worship God the Father alone.

> "You shall have no other gods before Me. You shall not make for yourself an idol in the form of anything in heaven above or on the earth beneath... You shall not bow down to them or worship them; for I, the Lord your God, am a jealous God..."
>
> (Exodus 20:3-5)

A compromise between Christianity and paganism is not worshipping God in spirit and truth, but is an unholy mixture – an abomination for the people of God and detestable to the Lord. In these last days, God is raising up a remnant of believers, both Jews and Gentiles, who understand the truth; who have heard the prophetic warning,

> "Come out of her, My people... Flee Babylon, or you will be swept away in her sins."
> (Rev. 18:4, paraphrase)

The Lord is soon preparing to return for a pure and holy virgin bride, not dragging one foot in Babylon and the other in God. The Lord is returning, not as the meek, sacrificial Passover lamb, led to the slaughter, but as the Lion of the tribe of Judah, to destroy the wicked of the earth, to judge the dead, and to establish His eternal Kingdom in the New Jerusalem. (Rev. 21, Zech. 14)

True Repentance Means Change

It is time to hear the prophetic warning, the call of the shofar, to repent and turn back to the ways of God. The time is now, to listen for the heartbeat of God –what would He have you do in these last days to prepare for His coming?

Many people, believe that all they need to do is recite a little prayer and Hallelujah, they are saved forever. The message of cheap grace preached from some church pulpits and over radio and T.V. is that once you have prayed a prayer of salvation, you are forever saved, and no matter what you do or how you behave, you will still end up a saint in heaven. This is why so much sin and immorality can exist in the Church.

I know of a married woman in a large, charismatic church who sang in the choir and attended services three times per week. She abandoned her husband and young children in order to commit adultery with a married man. We attended a prayer meeting here in the land of Israel where a man got up, lifted his hands and fervently blessed the congregation. Throughout the meeting, he sang and praised the Lord. The people called him their Christian brother. Later, we found out that this man had left his wife and eleven children to carry on an adulterous affair. When he comes home, he beats his wife. If the message of cheap grace is true, then these people have nothing to fear when they stand before God, the Judge. If all we need to do is 'believe in Jesus' and His blood allows us to continue sinning, then why not? They're 'saved', aren't they?

This is not what Yeshua Himself told us:

> **"Not everyone who says to Me, 'Lord, Lord,' will enter the kingdom of heaven, but only he who does the will of My Father who is in heaven. Many will say to Me on that day, 'Lord, Lord, did we not prophesy in Your name, and in Your name drive out demons and perform many miracles?' Then I will tell them plainly, 'I never knew you. Away from Me, you who practice lawlessness.'"**
>
> (Matthew 7:21-23)

Clearly, these people consider themselves Believers. Not only do they call Yeshua 'Lord', but they are also actively involved in church ministry, prophesying, casting out demons, and performing miracles, and yet Yeshua does not know them. He sends them away.

The Titanic and Grace

Many in the Christian Church can be compared to the Titanic. It was the arrogance of man that sank that great ship. They believed that nothing could sink it, not even God, and yet in His hands, it snapped like a thin toothpick and sank into the ocean deep.

Today, many believe that they are saved, no matter how they

live in ways contrary to God's Word. They think that they are above the laws of God, claiming, *"I'm not under the law"*. This verse actually states,

> **"For sin shall not be your master, for you are not under law but under grace."**
> (Romans 6:14)

This verse does not claim that because of grace we no longer need to keep the laws and commandments of God, but that His grace enables us to live in ways pleasing to Him, and to forsake sin – acting in ways that He hates.

According to the new covenant, God's law should be in our minds and written on our hearts.

> **"The time is coming,' declares the Lord, 'when I will make a new covenant with the house of Israel and with the house of Judah... I will put My law in their minds and write it on their hearts. I will be their God and they will be My people."**
> (Jeremiah 31:31-33)

This new covenant is not just for Israel and Judah, although it is also very definitely for them. The new covenant, sealed in the blood of Yeshua the Messiah is open to anyone. As New Covenant Believers, is it not time to allow for the painful process of circumcision to be performed on our hearts in order that the Holy Spirit may cause us to obey God's laws and commandments?

"I will give you a new heart and put a new spirit in you; I will remove from you your heart of stone and give you a heart of flesh. And I will put My Spirit in you and move you to follow My decrees and be careful to keep My laws."

(Ezekiel 36:26-27)

CHAPTER SEVEN

SIMCHAT TORAH

The three fall feasts of the Lord, Yom Truah, Yom Kippur, and Sukkot, are followed by a celebration called Simchat Torah, which means to rejoice in the Torah.

Often, the Hebrew word, Torah, is translated in our English Bibles as 'Law'. Therefore, we could say that this is a festival of rejoicing in the laws or commandments of God. Jews understand that God's Torah – His laws and commandments- are a 'tree of life' to us. The Torah contains all the wisdom and instruction we need to live a healthy, happy, successful lifestyle. The Lord said to Joshua,

> **"Be careful to obey all the law (Torah) My servant Moses gave you; do not turn from it to the right or to the left, that you may be successful wherever you go. Do not let this Book of the Law (Sefer Torah) depart from your mouth; meditate on it day and night, so that you may be careful to do everything written in it. Then you will be prosperous and successful."**
>
> (Josh. 1:7-8)

As the nation God initially chose to reveal His Torah to, giving them the mission to spread its light to every nation, the

Jewish people choose to set aside this specific day to 'rejoice in the Torah'. Most Christians I have encountered, however, sincerely believe that the Torah has been abolished with the crucifixion and resurrection of Jesus Christ, despite His own words to the contrary. While Christians dance and sing about their 'liberty in Christ' that supposedly allows them to transgress the Torah. How one can read the entirety of the bible and still carry this viewpoint is beyond me.

> **"Blessed are the undefiled in the way, who walk in the Torah of the Lord... Open my eyes that I may see wondrous things in Your Torah... You rebuke the proud – the cursed, who stray from Your commandments... For Your Torah is my delight..."**
>
> (Psalm 119:1, 18, 21, 70)

The Psalmist says,

> **"Indignation has taken hold of me because of the wicked, who forsake Your Torah."**
>
> (Psalm 119:53)

I feel the same when I hear of so many Christians who consider the 'Old Testament' (the Torah), as a sort of antiquated, fossilized, historical record. Worse yet is the arrogance it fosters that Christians are somehow 'superior' in their 'freedom from the law' than the 'less enlightened' Jews who still consider themselves 'under the law'. This is a major stumbling block between Jews and Christians.

The Holy Spirit, however, is moving! Many people's eyes are being opened to wondrous things in the Torah. If we see the Torah as an incredible gift and blessing from the Lord, we should be happy to share it with whomever asks to receive it, whether Jew or Gentile. Some people claim that the Torah is only for Jewish people, and that Gentiles are not 'required' to carry such a 'burden', but the Lord says that His commandments are not burdensome. They are the way to peace and blessing. Who are we, as Jewish believers, to keep it to ourselves and not share such a precious treasure with our Gentile brothers and sisters in the Lord? We should encourage, and not discourage those few brave souls who challenge the entire Christian status quo in learning about and then obeying the Torah.

Of course all of the words of the ancient Hebrew prophets can serve as a double-edged sword to convict us of sin. I sometimes wonder why God asked them to speak such a tough message to a people who didn't want to listen. But today, the Word of God is still alive through their writings and through the ministry of the Holy Spirit to lead and guide us into the truth. Jeremiah warned the people of God over and over again, but they considered themselves righteous because they went to the temple and the sacrifices were being made for their atonement.

> **"Do not trust in these lying words, saying, 'The temple of the Lord, the temple of the Lord, the temple of the Lord are these.'"**
>
> (Jeremiah 7:4)

We cannot sin, and then claim sanctuary by going to church, and saying we are delivered to do all these things because of the blood of Jesus.

> **"Will you steal, murder, commit adultery, swear falsely, burn incense to Baal, and walk after other gods whom you do not know, and then come and stand before Me in this house which is called by**

> My name, and say, 'We are delivered to do all these abominations'?"
>
> (Jeremiah 7:9-10)

No, we do not have liberty to do whatever we want, and still be saved 'by the blood of Jesus'. God says to Ephraim that they should go and look at what He did to His people Israel at Shiloh because of their wickedness. We can look at God's dealings with Israel as an example and a warning to us. If He did not spare them, the apple of His eye, His special treasured possession among the nations, why do we think He will spare us?

> **"Do not be haughty, but fear. For if God did not spare the natural branches, He may not spare you either."**
>
> (Rom. 11:20-21)

We would do well to heed this warning. God says that at some point, we can cross the line of grace, whereby no amount of intercession will avail.

> **"Therefore do not pray for this people, nor lift up a cry or prayer for them, nor make intercession to Me; for I will not hear you."**
>
> (Jeremiah 7:16)

People of God, we must get our lives right before God – now! The alarm of the shofar is sounding across the nations. The warning of the prophets declares, *"Repent and turn back to God."* If you have been convicted while reading this book, please remember that its purpose, as is any prophetic warning, is not to bring guilt and condemnation, but a 'Godly sorrow which leads to righteousness'. As Paul said,

> "Even if I caused you sorrow by my letter, I do not regret it. Though I did regret it – I see that my letter hurt you, but only for a little while – yet now I am happy, not because you were made sorry, but because your sorrow led you to repentance. For you became sorrowful as God intended and so were not harmed in any way by us. Godly sorrow brings repentance that leads to salvation and leaves no regret, but worldly sorrow brings death."
>
> (2 Corinthians 7:8-10)

Please seek the Lord now while He may be found. He is faithful to forgive the sins that we confess to Him in sincerity. He is close to those with a broken and contrite spirit. Pray from your heart forgiveness for those things that He reveals to you which are not pleasing in His sight. Be prepared to forsake them and walk in obedience to His Spirit. Seek for ways to make restitution for any wrongs committed by yourself or by those you represent (family, race, nation, etc.). Remember that we are children of God and have been granted liberty to come boldly to the throne of grace, covered in the blood of the lamb,

> "that we may obtain mercy and find grace to help in time of need."
>
> (Hebrews 4:16)

Observing even something as wonderful as the Torah of God without the life giving waters of the Holy Spirit soon degenerates into the dry desert of legalism. But Yeshua told us of the glorous hour when true worshipers would worship the Father both in Spirit and Truth. (John 4:23)

POSTSCRIPT
CELEBRATING THE FALL FEASTS

Tradition, tradition...(again-from Fidler on the Roof)

Many excellent books have been written specifically for the purpose of teaching people how to celebrate God's appointed times, and I do not intend to repeat their work. One caution I must strongly issue to those who want to begin celebrating the feasts is to distinguish between what is Biblically commanded and that which is simply Jewish tradition. Not that there is anything wrong with traditions, as long as we remain aware that tradition is not law. Yeshua said that some religious people transgressed the commands of God for the sake of their traditions. And worse yet, they taught their man-made rules as if they were doctrines of God. (Matt. 15:3,9) It seems to be a common trap for those zealous to begin celebrating the Feasts of the Lord to fall into legalism about the form of worship. For example, rabbinic tradition states that the sukkah must be built so that one can see the stars through the roof. Well, where in the Bible does it say that? Couldn't a tent suffice? It is definitely a temporary dwelling. At least it keeps people dry in the rain better than a structure with a leaky roof. We must not become so concerned with externals, since God cares more about what is going on in our hearts and our openness to His Spirit's workings in our lives. The celebration of these appointed times need not become a legalistic burden. There is much liberty for individual expressions of celebration and worship through the Spirit of Elohim (Ruach Hakodesh).

We are **"ministers of the new covenant, not of the letter but of the Spirit; for the letter kills, but the Spirit gives life....Now the Lord (Ha-Adon) is the Spirit, and where the Spirit of the Lord is, there is liberty."**
(2 Corinthians 3:6, 17)

May God bless you, and may the mourning and repentance of Yom Tru'ah and Yom Kippur be followed by the joy of our blessed hope in Sukkot – our God dwelling forever with us.

To contact the Author write:

Hannah Nesher, Voice for Israel
Suite #313- 11215 Jasper Ave.
Edmonton, Alberta
T5K 0L5 Canada

www.voiceforisrael.net

*Please include your testimony or help
received from this book when you write.*

Your prayer requests are welcome

Additional Teaching Materials by Hannah Nesher

DVDs

Shalom Morah I (Hebrew for Christians & Hebrew Names of God) 11 DVD set

Shalom Morah II (Hebrew for Christians & Wisdom in the Hebrew Alphabet) 10 DVD set

Exploring the Jewish Roots of the Christian Faith

Unity in the Messiah

Because He Lives

Messianic Jewish Wedding in Jerusalem

There is a God in Israel

Messianic Jewish Passover

Passover Lamb or Easter Ham?

Voice Out of Zion II (Where is Your Brother Jacob?)

Walking Through the Wilderness

Ruth: A Righteous Gentile

Messiah in Chanukah

BOOKS

Grafted in Again

Journey to Jerusalem

Come Out of Her My People

Messiah Revealed in Purim

Messiah Revealed in the Sabbath

Messiah Revealed in Passover

Messiah Revealed in Chanukah

Kashrut: The Biblical Dietary Laws

Messiah Revealed in Shavuot

You Know My Heart (English booklet)

You Know My Heart (Hebrew booklet)

www.ingramcontent.com/pod-product-compliance
Lightning Source LLC
LaVergne TN
LVHW051604070426
835507LV00021B/2753